pick up this book unless you have a couple of hours to spare—because once you start to read, you will be unable to put it down. And when you have finished, you will have gained important insights that will be of real use in your daily life. **Right Risk** is right on.

> —Michael J. Apter, Ph.D., author of
> *The Dangerous Edge*, and Director,
> Apter International, Inc.

I don't know anyone who lives a risk-free life so I can't think of anyone who would not find immediate value in this superb book on the truths and myths of positive risk-taking. Bill Treasurer uses his high-diving youth and life as an executive coach and transforms it into a hundred-foot-high platform of wisdom for us all.

> —John Shuster, author, *Answering Your Call*

Right Risk is right on. This wonderful book captured my total attention on the first page. I read it in one sitting and ordered copies for my friends. A great read written by a risk-taking, humble man.

> —Charlie Eitel, Chairman & CEO,
> The Simmons Company

Right Risk provides the first practical approach to making the most of one's self through not allowing yourself to become paralyzed by self-doubt and fear of failure. Treasurer not only speaks from real experience, but also shares the important successful risk-taking experiences of others that he encountered in business, in sport, and in his personal life!

> —Bob Carr, President of
> Executive Adventure

Bill shows us that risk taking is a skill, an important tool that, used correctly, will guide you toward living . . . not just existing. Even if you're not facing a risk at this moment, **Right Risk** can be a valuable weapon to be stored for the future . . . if you think you will not face risks in your future, then you need this book more than anyone.

> —Dustin Webster, 7 time World Cliff
> Diving Champion, Acapulco Cliff Diving
> Champion, RedBull Pro Athlete, and now
> . . . Right Risker

Right Risk

10 Powerful Principles for Taking Giant Leaps with Your Life

Bill Treasurer
(a.k.a. *Captain Inferno*)

Marie, Good Luck with all your Right Risks + Giant Leaps!

Bill Treasurer

BK®

BERRETT-KOEHLER PUBLISHERS, INC.
San Francisco

Berrett-Koehler Publishers, Inc.
235 Montgomery Street, Suite 650
San Francisco, CA 94104-2916
Tel: (415) 288-0260 Fax: (415) 362-2512   www.bkconnection.com

Quote from "Ripple," by Robert Hunter, copyright Ice Nine Publishing Company. Used with permission.

"Storm Windows," written by John Prine, ©1980 Big Ears Music (ASCAP) /Bruised Oranges Music (ASCAP)/Administered by Bug. All rights reserved. Used by permission.

Ordering Information
Quantity sales. Special discounts are available on quantity purchases by corporations, associations, and others. For details, contact the "Special Sales Department" at the Berrett-Koehler address above.

Individual sales. Berrett-Koehler publications are available through most bookstores. They can also be ordered direct from Berrett-Koehler:
Tel: (800) 929-2929; Fax: (802) 864-7626; www.bkconnection.com
Orders for college textbook/course adoption use. Please contact Berrett-Koehler: Tel: (800) 929-2929; Fax: (802) 864-7626.

Orders by U.S. trade bookstores and wholesalers. Please contact Publishers Group West, 1700 Fourth Street, Berkeley, CA 94710.
Tel: (510) 528-1444; Fax (510) 528-3444.

Berrett-Koehler and the BK logo are registered trademarks of Berrett-Koehler Publishers, Inc.

Printed in the United States of America

Berrett-Koehler books are printed on long-lasting acid-free paper. When it is available, we choose paper that has been manufactured by environmentally responsible processes. These may include using trees grown in sustainable forests, incorporating recycled paper, minimizing chlorine in bleaching, or recycling the energy produced at the paper mill.

Library of Congress Cataloging-in-Publication Data
Treasurer, Bill, 1962–
    Right risk : 10 powerful principles for taking giant leaps with your life /
Bill Treasurer.
        p. cm.
    Includes bibliographical references and index.
    ISBN 1-57675-246-1
    1. Risk-taking (Psychology) I. Title.
BF637.R57T74 2003
158.1—dc21   2003040376

FIRST EDITION
07 06 05 04 03   10 9 8 7 6 5 4 3 2 1

Contents

※

Foreword

by Larry Wilson

To me, the purpose of a book's Foreword is to give the reader a preview of what they can look "forward to" for investing their time and energy learning what the author is trying to communicate. Well, get ready for a big return on your investment.

You've heard that "When the student is ready, the teacher shows up"? Well, Bill Treasurer is the right teacher, for the right time, to help us get it right about Right Risk-taking. Like any good teacher, he's "been there and done that" when it comes to taking risks. More important, however, he's captured the right insights about risk-taking that we can all understand and apply to our own lives.

And why would we want to do that? Well, take a look out life's window today. The only thing that's certain is uncertainty. Nobody, and I mean nobody, has all the answers. It's all up for grabs, and the rewards will go to those who have learned how to thrive in all this ambiguity. Here, thriving is the effect. Risk-taking is the cause.

So, how does Right Risking fit into this new formula of success? For starters, we're heading down a new road where no man, woman, or child has ever been before. We're traveling into a future world of change that's changing differently than change has ever changed in the past. If you are not confused by it all, you're just not paying attention.

This new future is not entirely predictable. The best we can do is be prepared for it. We can no longer sit around waiting for somebody else to tell us "what's up" or what to do about it. They don't know the answer either. That means it's up to us to prepare ourselves.

And where did *you* learn to take risks? Did your Mom ever say, "Now go out and take some real risks today, honey, so you can prepare yourself for an uncertain future?" I don't think so. Did you learn risk-taking at school? I don't think so. Did your job, your boss, or your culture train you in the ten principles of Right Risk-taking? Again, I don't think so. What all of them gave you was plenty of advice on how to avoid risks, on how to "Play not to lose."

I've spent most of my work life attempting to help people overcome these early cultural mis-teachings. Some of the hardest risks we take are asking for help, saying we're sorry, or forgiving someone we believe did us in. It's big time risk-taking to change your career, to change your mind, or to change your responses to life. Any of these require Right Choices and Right Risks. Having the right coach to support you can really help. With Bill Treasurer and this book at your side, you'll find your way to choose growth over fear.

So, go ahead. Take the risk. Your life is worth it.

Larry Wilson,
founder of The Wilson Learning Group and
The Pecos River Learning Centers,
co-author of *Play to Win*
and *The One-Minute Sales Person*

Acknowledgments

This is the place I get to say "thank you" to all the people who have been instrumental in developing the book, while breathing a sigh of relief that the book is, whew, done. I like to think of it as a sort of "Amen," where the book gets blessed with an invocation of gratitude and humility, before I launch into a couple of hundred pages of less-than-humble opinionating.

On this day, I am especially thankful for the all the people who helped bring this book to life, including Marsh Ford, who proofread the first draft manuscript, and Olga Epstein, my researcher, proofreader, and candid thinking partner. Thanks also to the good folks at Berrett-Koehler Publishers for their hard work and for fighting to make the world of work a more humane place. This includes my review team who graciously reviewed my manuscript, as well as Detta Penna and Pat Brewer. A special thanks goes out to Steven Piersanti, Berrett-Koehler's president, for his exacting judgment and for taking a risk on me and my book.

I owe a debt of gratitude to all the people who shared their insights about risk with me, especially Dr. M. J. Apter, who spent two generous days with me musing about risk;

my former boss Hines Brannan, who has taken more than a few risks on me over the years, and taught me that disciplined risk-taking is smart business; and Father Vince Malatesta and actor Tom Key, who showed me how our faiths call us to take risks.

In a book on risk-taking, it is only appropriate that I thank the people who have taken some risks with me along the way: my buddy and fellow whitewater kayaker, Hal White, for his friendship and vast storehouse of hippie music; my coachees, who allowed me to work with them on the risks they faced in their lives; my mentor, O.K. Sheffield, Jr., for helping me take smarter risks than I used to; and all the former members of the U.S. High Diving Team, the craziest bunch of wingnuts I ever met (be thankful that I didn't share more about our wild escapades in this book!).

I am also thankful for the countless people who have had such a positive impact on my life, especially Dick Thompson, Bob and Anne Carr, and Dr. Marilyn Vickers. Thanks goes out as well to my friends at Leadership Strategies, Inc.; Learning Technologies, Inc.; Leadership Dynamics Inc.; and to my former colleagues at Accenture. Thanks also to my cohorts at Giant Leap Consulting, who exemplify our motto: *Daring To Excel*.

I am particularly thankful for Larry Wilson, a friend and kindred spirit, for writing the book's Foreword.

This book would not have been written were it not for my parents, who blessed me with an underdog spirit, my brother and sisters who provided unending encouragement, and my dog, Gulliver, who always takes my stress away.

My wife, Shannon, deserves special thanks, not only for her love and support but also for reminding me to, occasionally, "let-the-risk-thing-go." Were it not for her prodding me to walk the dog, rake the leaves, iron my shirts, etc., I am sure I would have fallen into a risk-obsessed lunacy. I love you, Shannon, for guarding my sanity.

Finally, I am grateful to be led by a Higher Power, who builds my confidence, gives me the strength to face fear, and allows me to live by Providence.

Bill Treasurer
Decatur, Georgia
April, 2003

*To Ford Winter,
my first diving coach,
for helping me take flight.*

Introduction: All Life Is Risk

To live is to risk. Risk-taking is as essential to life as breathing. It is the oxygen of such things as innovation, entrepreneurialism, leadership, wealth creation, and high adventure. Without risk, there can be no scientific progress, economic expansion, or community activism. At a more personal level, remove risk and there is no personal growth, career advancement, or spiritual development (faith, after all, is a big risk). Personally and collectively, all progress, advancement, and momentum depend on risk. Like air, it is both nourishing and life-sustaining. And, like change, risk is constant, inescapable, and inevitable.

To risk is to live. As a vehicle to personal progress, taking risks is the surest way to get from where you are to where you want to be. The most fulfilling times in your life—the times you felt most alive—have undoubtedly been when you surprised yourself by doing something you never imagined you could, something hard, something *scary*.

Though most of us have enjoyed the accompanying rewards of an intelligently taken risk, most of us have crashed-'n-burned under an ill-considered one as well. By definition, to face risk is to be vulnerable and exposed to harm. Consequently, we spend a lot of time trying to avoid risk by "playing it safe." Chances are, anytime you have passed up a big opportunity, stayed in an unsatisfying situation, or failed to stick up for yourself, avoiding risk had a lot to do with your behavior.

In a world that continually reminds us about how unsafe it is, it is difficult to maintain a "play it safe" approach. From terrorist threats, to stock market gyrations, to corporate implosions, we are buffeted by the reckless risks of others. In an increasingly compressed and frenetic world, we are like billiard balls being smacked around in somebody else's pool-hall hustle.

Ironically, those who play it safe may be in the greatest danger. When we don't take risks we get stuck in a rut of safety. Over time, we become trapped inside our own life, like a pearl confined to its shell. Life becomes stale and boring. We grow resentful at ourselves for letting our grand passions languish. We tell ourselves, *there's got to be something more out there for me*. But we know we'll never find it unless we take more risks.

Risk or Be Risked Upon

Given risk's inevitability and its central role in living a fulfilled life, combined with the realities of an increasingly risk-intense world, knowing how to take risks should be a part of everyone's core life curriculum. Rather than let risks be inflicted on you by happenstance, today's realities dictate that you learn to initiate them yourself. As a friend of mine likes to say, "You're either part of the bulldozer, or you're part of the pavement."

Fortunately, "being part of the bulldozer" does not mean you have to act like it. Unlike many of the risks that are imposed on you from the outside, the risks you take can be anchored to steadfast principles that serve to strengthen your life instead of undermine it.

What This Book Is About

Right Risk is about taking more deliberate and intentional risks in an increasingly complex world. It is about all the things that happen to you when you are planning for, engaging in, or running from, a risk. It aims to answer such questions as: How do I know which risks to take and which to avoid? How do I balance the need to take more risks with the need to preserve my safety? How do I muster up the courage to take risks when it is so much easier not to? How do I confront all those people who keep telling me what a mistake it would be to take the risk? And, most importantly, How do I make risk-taking less of an anxiety-provoking experience? (You'd probably take more risk if you just plain enjoyed it more, right?)

Right Risk aims to help you make smart and courageous choices, by taking risks that most reflect your personal value system, or what I call "Right Risks." Right Risks are as unique to the risk-taker as a fingerprint. They are those that, regardless of outcomes, are always deemed successful because they are taken with a clean conscience and clear calling. They are at once deliberate, life-affirming, and closely aligned with one's deepest core values. Right Risks stand for something.

We face Right Risk opportunities when deciding whether or not to get married, have children, or confront a loved one. Also whenever we are considering joining a social cause, converting to a different religious denomination, switching political parties, or marrying someone outside our own race or ethnicity. In our work lives we face Right Risk decisions when we grapple with whether to sign on for a position that is beyond our skills, accept an overseas assignment, expose a company impropriety, or elevate a groundbreaking but tradition-defying idea. For better or for worse, the choices we make in such instances can have enduring consequences.

If you are still unclear as to what this book is about, take a moment and reflect on these two things:

1. The greatest risk you've ever taken.

2. The risk you've always wanted to take but have been too afraid to do so.

In other words, this book is about *you* and the big risk decision that you are grappling with. To risk or not to risk, that is always the question.

What This Book Is *Not* About

Much of what has been written about risk deals with risk management and comes from actuaries and statisticians, primarily in the insurance industry. In that arena, risk is a four-letter word, a thing to be avoided, controlled, or reduced. It is dealt with rationally, impersonally, and with a great deal of caution. But it is a mistake to universally apply the risk management ethos to every risk endeavor. The question is: why are we taking all our advice about risk-*taking* from people who notoriously *avoid* risk? When we do, we put an overemphasis on the word *risk* often to the exclusion of the word *taking*, and our posture becomes one of risk avoidance. Isn't it time for a book about risk-taking written from a risk-taker's vantage point?

Right Risk offers a new set of risk-taking principles that aim to balance caution with courage, sensibility with spiritedness. Unlike risk management books, the emphasis here is on risk-*taking* as a verb, an action, something you do. Thus *Right Risk* comes with a new presupposition: that risk-*taking* is every bit as important, if not more so, than risk-*mitigation*.

How I Became Acquainted with Risk

I am an ordinary man who spent seven years taking extraordinary risks. From 1984 to 1991, leaping from risk's precipice was my job—literally. During that time, I performed over 1500 high dives from heights that scaled to 100 feet, while traveling throughout the world as a member of the U.S. High Diving Team. I am not an Olympian. Contrary to popular belief, high diving is not an Olympic sport. In the Olympics, the competition stops at 10 meters, roughly 33 feet. Our lowest high dive (to use an oxymoron) began at 60 feet, and most were performed at the life-threatening height of 27 meters, or roughly 100 feet. Last time I checked, the world record stood at 187 feet. The diver, a Swiss named Oliver Farve, broke his back in two places. High diving was an "extreme" sport before the term was coined.

The high dive was not the only risk my comrades and I took as part of an aquatic entertainment production. We also performed dangerous springboard stunts called *dillies*, dives that two divers perform together. Dillies are aerial acrobatics, like the "Horse & Rider," where one diver does a reverse somersault landing on the back of another in mid-air, or the "Baby Catch," where one diver runs into the arms of another, pushing both into a conjoined somersault, one flipping backward, the other forward. While dillies were crowd-pleasers, they were also dangerous. One misstep and both divers could end up in wheelchairs.

The best example of the extreme risks I took during my years as a high diver is the 300 dives performed as a petroleum-fueled alter ego. All forms of entertainment require a grand finale and ours was truly spectacular. Each evening we would dim the lights of the aqua-theater and await the arrival of a high-octane superhero who came dressed in a cape drenched with gasoline. With the striking of a match, an ordinary high diver was transformed into Captain Inferno, the human volcano! To confirm what you may have already suspected, that's me on the front cover of the book.

Other than a lingering case of swimmer's ear, a perpetually sore back, and a few photos of a svelte looking blonde guy who 30 pounds ago apparently used to be me, I have nothing tangible to show from my high-diving days. Instead, I am left with an intangible reward of far greater value: the knowledge of how to take a risk.

Spend time with anything long enough and its nature begins to reveal itself. Having spent 7 years diving off risk's high platform, I have become well versed in its ways. Like an idiot savant, I have a wealth of knowledge within a very narrow range. It just so happens, however, that the knowledge I do have is eminently useful to nearly everyone. Each of us faces a major risk at one time or another. In subsequent chapters, I will share with you some of the valuable lessons that I learned atop the high-dive ladder so that you can risk more confidently right here on the ground.

Fortunately, my experience is not limited to risk's outer fringes. Indeed, I have learned just as much about risk-taking as an organizational development professional as I have leaping from death-defying heights. First, as vice president of an Atlanta-based teambuilding company, I worked with more than 75 organizations and learned that the strongest teams are those whose members are willing to take physical and emotional risks together. Few things galvanize a team as much as a good old-fashioned challenge. Later, as a change management consultant, I helped tough-minded business executives leap off the platform of change. Sometimes these leaps were small, like helping an executive transition into a new job. Other times the leaps were large, like helping hundreds of employees transition to a new company. In all cases, though, the leap from one state of being to another involved people taking risks. These days, as President of Giant Leap Consulting, Inc., a company whose motto is *Daring to Excel*, I work with high-powered executives as they face the overwhelming challenges of today's unrelenting business environment. For them there are two primary goals: how to take the risks leadership demands, and how to get others to take smart risks to advance the goals of the organization.

The Risks You Take

Although the risks you may be facing may not be as death-defying as a high dive, they are undoubtedly just as fear-inducing. Each of us faces a high dive somewhere in our lives. The disquieting feelings a high diver experiences at the edge of the platform are the same ones felt by a person facing such life-changing decisions as whether to go back to school, have surgery, buy a house, or work through the hardships of a failing marriage. A high dive is certainly no more frightening than having to give a major presentation to your boss's boss, notify a customer that you will blow a delivery date, or inform the audit committee that your financials were off by a decimal point and you made a million dollar mistake. We all have our high dives to face, and we face them any time we are confronted with a decision of consequence.

I want you to take a risk. Given the fact that you purchased this book, I assume that you do too. To buy a book on risk-taking expecting not to take a risk would be akin to taking a picture of a rainbow with black and white film. You would get the picture but miss the point. It is the risk you are challenged with that will give this book context and make it come alive for you. To be clear, my aim is *not* to turn you into a risk daredevil. Reading this book might make you a better gambler, stuntperson, or freakshow performer, but that is not my goal. Rather, my aim is to help you take the risks that most reflect your principles and values. Thus to draw the most value from this book, keep in the forefront of your mind the one risk you have always wanted to take but thus far have not. In other words, what is *your* high dive? Everything you learn about risk in this book will be focused on two primary goals: helping you decide whether or not to take the risk and, if you choose to do so, how to take that risk smartly and confidently.

What's the Reward?

The most enticing risks are those that come with meaningful rewards, and this book is no different. By the time you reach the last page, it is my belief you will be more comfortable with the uncomfortable, more courageous in facing fear, more assertive in confronting others, and more able to accept and influence reality. In short, you will be more prepared to take the risks you've always wanted to take with greater focus, discipline, and maturity.

The quality of our lives improves in direct proportion to our ability to take on challenging risks. Consider this simple fact: No one ever achieved greatness without taking a risk. Pick up the biography of any leader, hero, or person of prominence, and you will likely find a pivotal moment in his or her life that hinged on a risk. Thus the greatest benefit of reading *Right Risk* may very well be an accentuation of your own greatness.

Warning: Hazards Ahead

A few words of caution. Risk-taking is perhaps the most experiential of all topics. It would be unauthentic to talk about risk and not to take a risk in the process. Hence, this book will provoke you, challenge your beliefs and convictions, and march past the barricades of your comfort zones. To remain true to its subject, *Right Risk* aims to be both threatening and upsetting. Risk, like a violent thug, does all these things. At the same time, *Right Risk* aims to help enrich your character, strengthen your courage and resolve, and develop your risk-taking capabilities. Risk, like a selfless mentor, does all these things too. Like risk itself, this book aims to be both frightening and inspiring.

How This Book Is Organized

The book's first part, *Risk Is Everywhere*, discusses why risk-taking is becoming an increasingly necessary skill for dealing with a risk-saturated world. *It's Risky Out There* looks at risk's growing ubiquity and intensity. *The Right Risk* provides some useful criteria to help you decide whether your risk is right or wrong.

At its core, this book is about an intense moment, your high-dive moment, your big risk. Accordingly, the 10 Principles of Right Risk address the things you can do *before, during,* and *after* the risk moment. Part Two, *Readying for the Risk,* focuses on what you can do to better prepare for your big moment. The principles introduced in this part are *Find Your Golden Silence, Defy Inertia, Write Your Risk Scripts,* and *Turn On the Risk Pressure.*

Part Three, *Relish the Moment,* is about dealing with, and even enjoying, the intense moment itself. The principles discussed here are *Put Yourself on the Line, Make Your Fear Work for You,* and *Have the Courage to Be Courageous.*

Part Four, *Commit to the Risk,* covers how you can increase your chances of success once you decide to pursue your risk. The principles offered in this part are *Be Perfectly Imperfect, Trespass Continuously,* and *Expose Yourself.*

The book's final part, *Reaping the Rewards of Right Risk,* looks at what you'll ultimately gain from being a Right Risk-taker: yourself.

The 10 Principles of Right Risk, along with the other topics, weave together to form a safety net that will allow you to risk more confidently. However, don't feel obliged to read them all in sequential order. You wouldn't be a risk-taker if you followed the rules all the time, right? So give yourself permission to do it your own way. Choose the principles that appear most relevant to you based on the risk you are facing. You may wish to reread some principles multiple times, others you will merely glance over. No matter. The principles are not building blocks. They are a means to an important end: to help you take your big risk.

A Final Word Before You Begin . . .

As noted by the book's subtitle, the principles introduced here are centered on helping you take "giant leaps with your life." However, not all giant leaps are taken off high platforms. Very often, giant leaps are small risk actions with big risk payoffs. For example, a number of years ago a friend of mine took a major leap of faith, he got married. But as he will tell you, the *real* giant leap took place a year before the wedding, when he took the risk of sending his ex-girlfriend an unusual card. She had broken things off sometime earlier, after growing frustrated with his unwillingness to commit. After spending over a year alone, and having no contact with his ex, he summoned up the courage to send the special card. What was it? An exquisitely crafted invitation . . . to their wedding . . . one year hence.

Sometimes, one small step for you may lead to one giant leap for your life.

Part One

Risk Is Everywhere

You can't escape it. It is all around you. Sometimes you can see it, say, in riveting moments of triumph or defeat. Other times it is invisible, like a nerve gas, slowly taking over your system. It can be benevolent or benign, invigorating or debilitating, life-affirming or life-ending. It is RISK, and it is everywhere.

Faced with the inevitability of risk, we are left with two basic ways of dealing with it: doing something or doing nothing. Depending on the circumstances, either approach can be appropriate. But know this, whichever approach you take, you'll be taking a risk. When you act, you might fail. When you don't act, you might miss out on a big opportunity.

This part looks first at risk's ubiquity. Like it or not, the world is becoming a riskier place to live. You'll read about some of the ways that risk is growing in both prevalence and intensity, on a global scale, affecting us on a personal level. This part also looks at what makes a risk "right." Be it in action, or in inaction, there is a right way and a wrong way to approach risk. You'll read about the defining characteristics of a Right Risk, so that you can begin to decipher whether your big risk is worth pursuing.

It's Risky Out There

꧁

West of Kilkenny, in the heart of southern Ireland, is the little town of Galmoy, the birthplace of my great-grandmother, Mary McCormack. A few years ago, during a visit to the Emerald Isle, my wife and I journeyed to the small thatch-covered home where Gandy, as we called her, was born.

Other than her thick Irish brogue, my memories of Gandy are vague. She died when I was 10 years old. Yet as I peered through the windows of the humble little dwelling, I felt strangely connected to her. I was moved with the profound recognition that, at great personal cost, had she not taken the risks that she took, I would not exist.

Mary McCormack was 17 years old when, from the bow of a steamship headed for America, she waved goodbye to her mother and father. She would never see them again.

My great-grandmother's big risk, though courageous, was by no means unique in our family. Her husband, my great-grandfather, himself a Norwegian immigrant, took on the risky profession of a New York cop. Later, my paternal grandfather took the risk of opening a business, an Esso station in Pelham, N.Y. Even the relationship of my parents was the result of a small, but ultimately enduring risk. They met on a blind date. Like all families, and like humanity itself, my family is connected through a long lineage of risks taken.

The Right Risk Question

Throughout the ages, the most basic problem shared by all people is knowing which risks to take, and which to avoid. Although the experience of struggling with a risk decision is both universal and unavoidable, the way each of us goes about deciding which risks to take is highly personal. Each of us takes risks for our own reasons and rationale. When faced with a risk, each of us is left to answer for ourself this simple, but profound, risk-discerning question: *Is this the right risk for me?*

Risks that are right for us may seem absurdly dangerous and completely unnatural to the spectator, making it difficult for them to support us. But when a risk is right for us, the real harm comes in letting it pass us by. Every risk can be split in two, the risk of action and the risk of inaction, and both have consequences. Had my great-grandmother stayed safe and sound in the sleepy little town of Galmoy, for example, she may have pleased her parents, but she would have had to carry the lifelong burden of a stillborn dream.

It is a mistake to think that Right Risks are danger free. "Right" is not a function of safety, it is a function of compatibility. The Right Risk for you may be entirely wrong for someone else. "Right" is in the eye of the beholder. I am sure that young Mary McCormack was viewed by some as crazy, perhaps even disloyal, for leaving home. But because Right Risks are organic to our own life, the unnatural act becomes the most natural choice for our own progression. With all the runaway irrationality of eloping lovers, when a risk is right for us, we won't let reason get in the way of passion.

Regardless of how unnatural or absurd they may seem to the outsider, Right Risks are those that are in our life's best interest. To say "yes" to a Right Risk is to promote your own development. Thus, when faced with a major risk, accurately answering the question *Is this the Right Risk for me?* becomes critically important to our life's progression.

A World of Risk

Risk-taking is closely tied to decision-making because it involves rendering a yes/no verdict between staying the same or changing. Our risks nearly always boil down to deciding between should I or shouldn't I, can I or can't I, will I or won't I. Each selection can make us more powerful or sink us deeper into victimhood. Making these straightforward, yet life-altering, decisions requires focused thinking and sound judgment. However, the complexities of the modern age are making it difficult to answer the right risk question with any degree of accuracy. The distractions and diversions of today are infringing on our ability to make good choices. While the proliferation of technology has allowed us to become continuously connected to each other, we have become entirely disconnected from ourselves.

At work or at home, 24/7/365, we are on call, on hold, or online. We have become a Society of The Perpetually Distracted, the result of which is an erosion of our intuitive powers of discernment and discrimination. We are becoming a world of fragmented thinkers, and fragmented thinking makes for ill-considered choices. Consequently, our Right Risk decisions often end up being made in a careless or reckless way. Risk appears to be getting riskier.

Although the technology-driven distraction of today is impeding our ability to make good risk choices, it hasn't stopped us from taking risks. Evidence suggests that, on a global scale, risk-taking is becoming more prevalent and extreme. Consider, for example, these barometers of our increasingly risky behavior:

- We are progressively willing to assume more risks with our money. In 2000, some 80 million people in the United States owned stocks (roughly 50% of households), more than at any time in the history of the stock market.[1]

- In the United States, there has been a huge expansion of legalized gambling, including pari-mutuel race-tracks, televised mega-buck lotteries, riverboat gambling, and Indian and non-Indian casinos. All but two states now have some form of legalized gambling.[2]

- People are increasingly willing to assume the risks of living beyond their means. Data from Australia, Britain, and Singapore all show a sharp rise in credit card debt.[3] In the United States, the amount of credit card debt held has tripled during the last decade to more than $700 billion![4] And the future looks no better. Credit card use among U.S. college students has skyrocketed. By senior year, 96% of students own credit cards, and the average number of credit cards held is 6.13.[5]

- Globally, the relative force and intensity of amusement park roller coasters grows yearly. In 1994 the top speed was 80 mph. In 2002 it was 107 mph.[6]

Not surprisingly, along with the growth in prevalence and intensity of risk has come an associated growth in the collateral damage that usually accompanies it. Consider these disturbing facts:

- In the two and a half years following the burst of the dot-com bubble, U.S. stock market losses were estimated to be $8.5 trillion.[7]

- In 1998 alone, some $50 billion was lost on legalized gambling in the United States, a figure that has grown (mostly in double digits) every year for nearly two decades.[8]

- The number of Americans declaring personal bankruptcy has risen from 284,517 in 1984 to a record of almost 1.5 million in 2002.[9]

- According to conservative estimates from the U.S.

Consumer Products Safety Commission, the number of amusement park accidents grew from 3,419 in 1996 to 6,594 in 2000.[10]

What's Going On?

The human condition has always been imbued with risk, but a number of converging factors appear to be acutely intensifying our risk-taking behavior. These factors include boredom, a virtual backlash, risk availability, and the reach for the extreme.

Furious Boredom

Boredom has always been the prime instigator of risk-taking. The philosopher Schopenhauer noted that boredom is worse than suffering to the human condition. But what is unique about the boredom of our age is that it may be the result of being entirely too busy. The great paradox of the modern age is that people are overworked but bored. According to the International Labor Organization, on average, Americans work more than 1,979 hours a year. That is 137 more than Japan, 260 more than Britain, and 499 more hours than Germany. The average workweek for most professionals is 48 hours per week, a figure that scarcely reflects the amount of time people actually spend working because people are increasingly using their time off to get caught up with work.[11] A survey of 2,200 U.S. professionals conducted in March 2002 by Linkage, Inc., a corporate training company, found that 97% of the respondents reported doing job-related work on their vacations and days off, suggesting that we are never not at work.[12] This is compounded by the fact that Americans take fewer vacation days than any industrialized nation.[13] Yet, despite the frantic pace, most people are entirely sedentary all day long. The cubicle has become the modern-day salt mines. For many, work amounts to little more than being tethered to a computer, cranking out a rapid succession of deliverables. While everything is "rush

rush," the only things moving faster are our fingers tapping on the keyboard. Though mentally exhausted, our spirits and bodies thirst to feel alive again. According to one study of 2,500 people, despite living in truly remarkable times, 71% yearned for more novelty in their lives.[14] More and more people are taking risks to turn up the tempo of their lives.

Virtual Backlash

In times gone by, reality was just reality. The more "virtualized" our world becomes, the more people long for a more direct and authentic experience of what is real. Not simulated real, not virtual real, but REAL real. In a world where people communicate in cyberspace chat rooms, send mail through electronic bits and bytes, play "shoot 'em up" at the video arcade, get job training through computer simulation, and are entertained by "reality" television, risk-taking serves as a reality check. When the risks you take are simulations of the real thing, so too are the dangers. While a computer interface can approximate a risk, there are no real consequences for failure, and the experience falls flat. For pure danger-induced excitement, the joystick can't match the stickshift.

Unfettered Access to Risk

Today's risk-takers simply have more access to more intense risk experiences. One reason is the explosive growth of the adventure travel industry, which now generates some $110 billion in annual sales within the United States and, according to the Travel Industry Association of America, is the fastest growing segment of the $500 billion leisure travel market.[15] Nearly 10,000 tour operators offer everything from whitewater rafting trips in the Andes to submersible voyages to the bottom of the ocean floor off the coast of Europe.

Indeed, "cool" risk experiences have become the status symbol of the 2000s. The more outlandish the risk experience, the greater the bragging rights. For less than $15,000 you can brag about traveling at twice the speed of sound while cruising at 85,000 feet in a Soviet-made MiG-25 fighter jet. And for $59,000 you can gloat to your friends about your excursion to the top of Mount Everest (provided that you live to tell about it).[16] Furthermore, our access to risky endeavors is likely to grow. Now that Dennis Tito has broken the stratospheric ceiling by becoming the first civilian to visit the International Space Station (at a personal cost of $20 million), the sky's unlimited for our access to risky experiences.[17] Outer space is not just for astronauts anymore.

All That's Left Are Extremes

It takes a lot more these days to accomplish something truly extraordinary. 2002 marked the 75th anniversary of Charles Lindbergh's historic solo flight across the Atlantic. In an act of homage, his grandson Erik Lindbergh repeated the feat. 2003 marked the 50th anniversary of the first successful Mount Everest climb. To celebrate the occasion, the sons of Edmund Hillary and Tenzing Norgay went back to the mountain. In both instances the key word is *repeat*. Today's risk-taker contends with the fact that much of what is grand and gallant has been conquered numerous times over. The remaining choice is to repeat someone else's achievement or attempt more extreme stunts.

For example, in 1960 Joseph W. Kittinger Jr., a test pilot with the U.S. Air Force, became a legend among skydivers by parachuting from 102,800 feet. Just how will this amazing feat be eclipsed? By going to extremes, of course. Cheryl Stearns, a member of the Army's elite skydiving team, the Golden Knights, is planning on breaking Kittinger's record by taking a weather balloon 130,000 feet into the stratosphere—over 24 miles—and skydiving back to earth at speeds in excess of 800 mph.[18] When there is nowhere else to go, we go to extremes.

Today's extremism can also be seen in the popularity of such television shows as *Fear Factor*, *Survivor*, and the Fox Cable Network's *54321*, a nightly program dedicated entirely to extreme sports. In addition, *The X Games*, ESPN's veritable Olympics of extreme sports, are now telecast to over 180 countries.[19] But extremism transcends our recreational preferences. These are immoderate times, from gluttonous fast-food consumption, to radical forms of cosmetic enhancement (i.e., Botox), to gangsta-rap lyrics that make the Rolling Stones sound parochial. In today's world, contentment is found on the fringes.

Risk Is Always There

Though risk may be easiest to observe in macro level trends, it often hides unseen in the normal routine of our everyday lives. Risk is ever-present but only noticed when we stop to think about it. Consider the risks you face in your own life:

- Do you regularly drive 10 mph over the speed limit? While talking on a cell-phone?

- Do you smoke?

- Are you obese or overweight?

- Did you ever care for someone with a communicable disease?

- Did you ever engage in risky or unprotected sex?

- Have you ever converted from one religious or political belief system to another?

- Did you ever move away from home?

- Have you ever left one career for an entirely different one?

- Have you ever strongly disagreed with your boss but bit your lip and said nothing?

- Is there something that you really want to do but fear has prevented you from doing it?

As your answers likely suggest, almost everything we do (or fail to do), on some level, involves a risk. Whether it is leaving home, fighting for our beliefs, confronting the schoolyard bully, or simply trying something new, risk-taking is as elemental to life as inhaling and exhaling. Yet, given risk-taking's central role in the human experience, it is strange that there is no guide for improving one's risk-taking abilities. Instead, we are left to grope through our risk experiences like mapless explorers.

Someone Had To Do It

We live in a risk-saturated world. Rather than wit for risk to be inflicted upon us, we should press our chest against risk's bow, and wave goodbye to the safe shores of sameness with all the anguished optimism of an immigrant headed to a new world. Risk is, and always has been, our vehicle to the future. I have written *Right Risk* to help you face your risks squarely and intentionally, so that you can take the risks that are right for you. By drawing on the experiences of successful (and not-so-successful) risk-takers, as well as my own experiences at the extreme edge of risk (which you'll read about in the next chapter), I have created 10 Right Risk principles that provide a map for helping you navigate through your risk endeavors. Not only will following these principles make your risks more successful, on balance, they will make them more enjoyable as well.

I believe there is a right way and a wrong way to pursue a risk. The wrong way doesn't always lead to failure or injury, but it always leads to regrets. The right way, conversely, doesn't always lead to success or safety, but it is always regret free. The risks we regret the least, Right Risks, are those that uphold our principles. They are those that have been taken only after a careful evaluation of our skills relative to the riskiness of the situation. Thus, before moving on to the next chapter, please consider the following questions:

- How has risk been an essential part of your family's history?

- How is your world riskier today than it has been in the past?

- What is the big risk you are currently faced with?

- What factors have caused the risk to emerge at this point in your life?

- Why haven't you taken this risk yet? What is standing in the way of your pursuing this risk?

- In what ways is this risk similar to other risks you have faced in the past? How did those risks pan out? What lessons from those past risks might you be able to draw upon to help you face your current risk?

Right Risk

❋

California was the highest, over 100 feet. In Iowa, the roaring heartland winds nearly blew me off the ladder. In Germany, I kicked snow off the platform with my bare feet. The pool in Georgia was only 8 feet deep. In Saskatoon, Canada, the unheated water was in the low 40s. It rained the whole season in Seattle. I loved doing it at night in South Carolina. Virginia required a lot of aspirin. But it all started back in Texas.

A high diver remembers his first dive with the same fondness as other firsts in life—the first kiss, the first time you drive a car, the first time you buy a six-pack of beer, and the night you give your virginity the heave-ho. All of these inaugural events have one thing in common—a pounding heart. In Texas, my heart pounded like a judge's gavel.

Most high divers perform their first high dive during practice. I, however, had decided to perform my maiden high dive during our show in front of a live audience of 2,000 Texans. I had been inching toward this moment for weeks. High divers do not start at the top, they start at the bottom. Each day during practice, my teammates and I would goad each other, leaping from incrementally higher heights—first 10 feet, than 20, and so on. Now, after doing a practice dive at 60 feet, our team captain felt I was ready to take it up to 90 feet, almost three times higher than the top platform in the Olympic games.

My moment had arrived. Under the sweltering Texas sun, I grabbed the steel of the high-dive ladder. The higher I climbed, the more nervous I became. The body has a way of resisting foolishness. My palms tingled with sweat. My stomach teemed with rioting butterflies. I could hear the thumping of my pulse. Although I had performed scores of dives at lower levels, this was feeling more and more like an unnatural act. Men don't come equipped with wings.

At 60 feet I made a major mistake—I looked down. Suddenly, I was struck with paralyzing fear. "Oh God," I groaned, "this is the stupidest thing I've ever done. I should turn back now while I can still get out of this alive." The absurdity of the moment was head-spinning. What was I trying to prove? Was I really doing this to conquer my secret fear, or was it something else?

After a few deep breaths, I started to regain my composure. Somewhere inside me a little voice reasoned, "You can do this. You've visualized this moment over and over, you've practiced long and hard, and you've got a lot of support down there on the pool deck. Press on." With that, I swallowed hard, looked up at the top platform, and followed the assurances of my inner voice.

My back was to the audience as I situated myself on the top platform. To heighten the dramatic impact, a diver does not turn to face an audience until they are on the edge of their seats. As our team captain would say, "We want 'em frog tight with anticipation." This interlude of theatrical suspense allowed me to catch my breath and view the expansive Texas horizon. It was stunningly beautiful.

Then I heard Ben, our emcee, announce to the audience, "Ladies and Gentlemen, when Bill turns around, let's all put our hands together to wish him good luck on his very first high dive." That was my cue. When I turned around, the audience went wild. Texas crowds were raucous anyway, but the novelty of it being my first high dive made them especially rowdy. As the applause quieted, an anxious hush fell over the aqua-theater. It was all up to me, and I was scared to death. A flurry of thoughts and feelings bombarded me. "I could die. I could literally be dead in a few moments. Or maybe I will crash hard and be paralyzed. I'll be in a wheel-chair for the rest of my life." The fear was gripping, yet strangely exciting. This was, by far, the greatest risk I had ever attempted. It was a sheer rush teetering at the far edge of my own potential. It was also humbling. Of all the people who have ever lived, some 100 billion of them, there were probably fewer than 1,000 who had done what I was about to do. In a few moments, I would be one of them—dead, par-alyzed, or otherwise.

As I stretched out my arms and readied for the dive, it was as if my body had become the fulcrum between the poles of fear and desire: fear of what could go wrong and desire to succeed. It was an odd, balanced moment, a moment perfectly situated between past and future, surren-der and pursuit. It was a NOW moment. Confronting my own mortality made me feel wonderfully alive and fully immersed in the present. I was filled with supersensory awareness. I could see for miles and miles. I could feel the wind blowing between my fingers. And just above my head, on the top of the high-dive ladder, I could hear the American flag proudly snapping in the Texas wind.

Then the little voice whispered again, "You *can* do this." With that, I jumped off the ladder as if I were leaping into the arms of God.

For a fraction of a second—the instant between the dive's pinnacle and descent—I was suspended in mid-flight like a swan hovering near heaven's ceiling. Then, *schwoosh*, I started plummeting toward the water at breakneck speed. I had an overwhelming sensation that at any moment I would tumble out of control like a wayward lunar module. It looked as if the water was racing toward me with accelerat-ing velocity, though the reverse was true: I was moving toward *it* at nearly 50 mph. Yet the feeling that eclipsed all others was a profound vulnerability—that I was exposed. And I was. High divers do not wear protective padding; they wear swimsuits. You are completely unprotected.

The sensation of vulnerability was intensified by the knowledge that, once I left the platform, there was no turning back. There are, after all, no such things as air-brakes. So if I *did* go out of control, corrections were nearly impossible, and the consequences were life-threatening. Thus, the leap taken was full of fear.

As I careened toward the water, my body instinctively stiffened to prepare for impact. BAM! It felt as if someone had smacked the soles of my feet with a two by four. The impact was shuddering, as if every bone and tendon were being compressed and stretched at the same time. Then the water pummeled my chin with a bruising uppercut. Under the water, I literally shook my head in bewilderment. "Holy shit!" I thought as my brain scanned my body through a lightning-fast checklist. Arms? Check. Legs? Check. Back? Check. Neck? Check. Everything checked, I was okay . . . and profoundly grateful to be alive.

As I surfaced the water, fist raised in a sign of triumph, the audience's exuberance was matched only by the grin on my face. I had done it! I had faced my secret fear and done it! I had become a high diver.

Fifteen hundred high dives later, just writing about it gets my heart pounding.

Why on Earth Would You Do That?

High diving has been called a testament to man's indulgent pursuit of the insignificant. The risks my teammates and I took are easily misinterpreted as reckless folly. What did it prove, after all? That we could withstand 2.5 seconds of plummeting hell? So what? Questions of this sort have been asked of all risk-takers at one time or another. These questions imply that risks of this nature, which demand such a significant personal investment, have no redeeming value. Moreover, such risks defy both logic and biology. Self-preservation is, after all, the most basic desire shared by all living things. What sense does it make to purposely threaten your own safety and well-being just for a thrill?

Perhaps the best answer lies in George Mallory's famous reply when asked why he wanted to climb Mount Everest:

"Because it's there." To me, *it* means more than the mountain's location. *It* is all the lessons to be gleaned by going through the ordeal of taking a risk. *It* is the gratification derived from learning character-building lessons about fortitude, courage, sacrifice, and persistence. *It* is the wisdom gained from learning that satisfaction is on the far end of suffering. *It* is the personal fulfillment you feel when you withstand strength-sapping pain and find out what you are truly made of. *It* is the inexhaustible reward of learning to trust the dignified voice of your inner advocate. *It* is the spirit of adventure, the feeling of being fully alive. And ultimately, *It* is the self-confidence gained from experiencing firsthand the preeminent value of your own worth. *It* is all there for the taking if you are willing to take a risk. Mallory was right-we take risks because *IT* is there!

Where Risks Come From

At this point you may be wondering how, exactly, a high dive qualifies as a Right Risk. Perhaps it would help if I let you in on a little secret. I am afraid of heights. Ever since I was a little boy, my knees have weakened whenever I breathed the thin air of high places. Once when visiting the Empire State Building, as other brave souls peered over the guardrail gawking at the miniature metropolis below, I stood frozen and ashamed, my back pressed firmly against the concrete wall. Thus for me, taking a high dive was more than an act of bravado or a flight of fancy, it was an act of liberation from my fears and limitations. Right Risks usually are.

Notice I said I *am* afraid of heights. Even becoming a high diver did not fully conquer this fear. It did, however, help me build enough confidence to weaken fear's power over me. During my honeymoon, for example, I was able to lean against the guardrail of the Eiffel Tower with my wife, Shannon, and enjoy the breathtaking Parisian view. This illustrates the additive benefits of taking risks: Risk-taking in one area of your life can give you the confidence to live all of life more fully. Had I not taken my first high dive, I might never have enjoyed that romantic moment with my wife high above Paris.

A high diver who is afraid of heights is less unusual than you may think. The risks you are likely to be confronted with (and sometimes dangerously enamored with) are often solutions to your own internal dilemmas. Like nasty demons and faithful dogs, risks seek us out. They often bear the seeds of our own development by confronting us with situations that can only be successfully navigated by addressing our fears, weaknesses, or imperfections. Hence, risk is something we want and do not want at the same time. We are tempted by risks because they offer rewards that are compensatory to our inadequacies. But because they involve our fears, we are also repelled by them. Thus the risks confronting the stingy are often those demanding generosity, the risks confronting the irresponsible are often ones entailing responsibility, and the risks confronting the coldhearted are often those requiring compassion. And for folks who are afraid of heights? High dives.

Practical Matters

A few years ago, after giving a presentation on purposeful risk-taking to 300 software developers, one of the audience members came up to me and said, "You know, Bill, I appreciate your message about taking the risk of following one's passion, but the fact is, I have children to feed. Sure, I'd like to give up everything and become a blues singer, but let's face it, it wouldn't be practical." He was right, it wouldn't.

In a word, practical matters *matter*. Life's realities often make taking a risk just too plain risky. You and your spouse may decide to quit the rat race and head up to Vermont to open a quaint B&B, but if you haven't saved any money and you don't know the least little thing about running an inn, not only will you lose your B&B, you'll lose your shirt as well. Lack of time, money, knowledge, and support are all practical realities that risk-takers need to respect. Yet the proper function of what is *practical* is to serve what is *possible*. Thinking through practical matters makes for a richer and more sober evaluation of the risk. But when the practical subjugates the possible, our dreams become hostage to rationality. Sometimes practicality is just a plausible excuse for not risking. Human development is a function of risk-taking, and we mature, stagnate, or regress, according to our ability to risk deftly. By not risking, we face the supremely dangerous risk of personal entropy. Thus, to accommodate both the practical and the possible, the Right Risk-taker follows this simple rule: *respect* the practical, *revere* the possible.

The Myth of the Universal Risk-Taker

For convenience, it is tempting to sort people into two sweeping categories: risk-takers and risk-avoiders. But stereotyping people into *those who do* and *those who don't* is simplistic and leads to what I call The Myth of the Universal Risk-Taker. The underlying assumption being that the Universal Risk-Taker takes risks in every area of his or her life. Poke the assumption, however, and it falls apart.

For example, a hardnosed colleague of mine can fire a mediocre employee with ease, yet she is afraid to get on an escalator. My former boss could confidently give a presentation to 300 people, yet she was unusually awkward in small group settings. A close friend of mine is a federal agent and makes his living "running-n-gunning" on the streets of Newark, N.J., yet he has difficulty telling his wife he loves her because it makes him feel all squishy inside. Even my grandmother, who never shied away from taking the risk of expressing a bold opinion, could never muster up the courage to learn how to drive. In truth, everyone is both a risk-taker and a risk-avoider; we just take or avoid risks in different domains, be it physical, intellectual, interpersonal, or emotional. This is an important point, because you can borrow from the parts of your life where you are already taking risks to help build confidence in the areas where you are avoiding them.

While there is no Universal Risk-Taker, clearly some people are more inclined to take risks than others. Recent research suggests that attraction to risk may be a function of genetics. Two studies, one in the United States and the other in Israel, simultaneously researched the link between risk and genetics, and both reached the same conclusion: risk attraction can be explained genetically in about 10% of the population. In both studies, volunteers donated blood samples for DNA analysis and then completed surveys to assess their personality temperament. Respondents who scored high on novelty-seeking (a traditional measure of risk-taking) were also found to have a slightly longer form of a dopamine receptor gene that regulates the neurotransmitter dopamine. Dopamine is a powerful opiate-like substance produced by the brain that controls, among other things, the ability to experience pain and pleasure. The research suggests that a biological predisposition may account for at least some people's risk-taking behavior. This is true regardless of sex, race, or ethnicity.[1]

That genetics plays a part in risk-taking is not surprising. Our prehistoric ancestors needed to take risks in order to survive. Our earliest artistic images, the 32,000-year-old paintings on the walls of the cave dwellings in Chauvet, France, show a world teeming with dangerous beasts. Parading across the cave walls are bears, reindeer, bison, mammoths, lions, rhinoceros, wild mustangs, and raging bulls. Such a world demanded a willingness to confront harsh elements, explore new territories, and test which foods were safe or unsafe. This spirit of risk-taking, though stronger in some more than others, is part of everyone's heritage, not just some idealized Universal Risk-Taker.

So What Exactly Is Right Risk?

Regardless of how genetically predisposed a person is to taking risks, risk-taking success is contingent upon a good fit between the risk and the risk-taker. The risk-discerning question *Is this the Right Risk for me?* is really one of compatibility. Right Risks are often those that offer the potential to fill our gaps. Behind every Right Risk is a right reason, and successful risk-takers take the risks they do because the risks complete them in some way. Making those 1500 leaps off the high-dive platform taught me that risk-taking is not about seeking thrills, it is about seeking fulfillment.

Not Gratuitous Risk

Admittedly, some people are addicted to excitement. However, adrenaline junkies are generally not Right Risk-takers. Taking a risk just to get your jollies is the hallmark of gratuitous risk, not Right Risk. Gratuitous risk can be thought of as *risk for kicks*, and it serves little purpose beyond itself. Going skinny-dipping, streaking across campus, or "borrowing" a car for a joyride may keep one from being bored, but little else. More often than not, gratuitous risks are driven by whimsy or impulsiveness; while fun, they are largely superfluous.

Not Ego-Based Risk

Some people take risks to feed their egos. Ego-based risk-takers preoccupy themselves with one question: *What's in it for me?* The operative words here are "for me." Ego-based risk-takers are utterly self-serving. As long as the risk makes them rich, makes them a celebrity, or protects their image, it matters little if it does so at someone else's expense. What matters most, they think, is that in this dog-eat-dog world, they get their share.

Ego-based risk-takers view risk as a win/lose proposition, swaying back and forth between the magnetic fields of *desire for gain* and *fear of loss*, conditions that dictate most of their risk-taking actions. Just as often they will take risks because they stand to gain something as because they are afraid to lose something. Let's remember that as many people joined the dot-com hallucination because they did not want to lose out as because they wanted to strike it big.

. . . But Right Risk

Unlike risks of a gratuitous kind, Right Risks are deliberate, focused, and rich with meaning. Unlike ego-based risks, they transcend the bipolar fields of gain and loss, and are instead anchored to a higher purpose. Rather than feed one's ego,

Right Risks strengthen one's character. They are fulfilling not because they are fun and exciting (although they often are), and not because they are materially rewarding (although they can be), but because they transport us from where we are to where we want to be.

Right Risks are directed toward a specific destination— our better selves. In this way, Right Risks are often the means to an altruistic end. If, by taking a Right Risk, I become a better, more confident and integrated person, then I am better able to serve you, defend you, and build you up. For example, Sir Edmund Hillary's legacy is made all the greater because, along with climbing Mount Everest, he also helped build 27 schools and 2 hospitals for the Himalayan people.[2]

Obviously, not every extreme risk-taker takes Right Risks. A person may go bungee jumping for a multitude of reasons, including: to be cool (ego), to be thrilled (gratuitous), to be on the cover of a magazine (ego), "just because" (gratuitous), to overcome a debilitating fear (Right Risk), or to raise money for Orphans of Bungee Jumping (Right Risk). While it may be tempting to judge who is and who is not a Right Risk-taker, since only the risk-taker knows the true motivation for taking the risk, the Right Risk distinction is better left to the individuals themselves. Furthermore, not every risk needs to be a Right Risk. Sometimes we just want to stir things up, have a little fun, and live dangerously. Sometimes we want to live unhinged from any responsibility to which a Right Risk might oblige us. Life would be pretty dour were this not the case. If every risk taken were a Right Risk, one could easily slip into self-righteousness, that filthy condition that is itself ego-based (I am better, purer, or holier than you).

We often see Right Risks embodied by adventurers, explorers, and pioneers. But just as often, we see them personified by protesters, activists, and whistleblowers. Right Risks are just as much the domain of charitable workers, caretakers, and teachers, as they are the domain of entrepreneurs, innovators, and venture capitalists. They are taken regularly by artists and soldiers, scientists and priests. Just what do we mean by Right Risk? Many things. It can mean not taking action when we would rather take it, or taking action when we would rather not. Sometimes it means being well behaved, more often it means being misbehaved. It can mean acting out of levelheaded calculation, or lionhearted courage. One thing is sure, Right Risk nearly always means taking a risk despite the fact that you are afraid, vulnerable, and exposed.

The Hallmarks of Right Risk

More specifically, the four hallmarks of Right Risk are:

1. **Passion:** Right Risks are risks we care about intensely. Right Risks are often ordeals, and ordeals involve suffering. The word passion comes from the Latin verb *pati*, literally translated as "to suffer." By arousing the strongest, most untamed parts of our nature, and stirring up the wild mustangs in our soul, our passion gives us the raw energy and wherewithal to suffer through the anguishing moments that often accompany Right Risks.

2. **Purpose:** A Right Risk is taken out of a deep sense of purpose. Purpose serves to harness the wild horses of our passion and give them direction. Right Risks are rich with meaning. They stand for something beyond sensory or ego gratification. Rather than ask *Will it feel good? What will I get?* or *What will I lose?* the Right Risk-taker asks *How will this risk make me a more complete person?* and *How will this risk further my life's purpose?*

3. **Principle:** Right Risks are governed by a set of values that are both essential and virtuous. As mentioned, risks are essentially decisions, and when facing a decision of consequence, principles form a set of criteria against which the risk can be judged. The principles Right Risk-takers often use as the basis of their decision-making include, truth, justice, independence, freedom, mercy, compassion, and responsibility.

4. **Prerogative:** Right Risk-taking involves the exercise of choice. Right Risk-takers view the power to choose as a privilege and honor it as such. By consistently making choices that, at a conscious level, are aligned with their purpose and principles, they are better able to make superior judgment calls at an instinctual level—even in fast-moving situations.

In my consulting practice, I am often asked, "How will I know if the risk I am facing is a Right Risk?". I am always tempted to answer "You will know when you know." People seem to want to hurry through the risk experience and just jump to its conclusion. But answering the Right Risk question *Is this the Right Risk for me?* requires depth of thought. It is unlikely that you'll be able to answer the question quickly. Nevertheless, I usually instruct people to use the four P's. If your risk is something that arouses your spirit (passion), if the risk will help you progress to some higher order goal (purpose), if it is anchored to deeply rooted values that you hold dear (principles), and if you will be deciding to pursue the risk of your own free will (prerogative), the chances are, it is a Right Risk.

An Example of Right Risk

In early 1960, Dr. Frances Kelsey was given her first assignment as a new employee with the FDA. After being on the job for only one month, she was asked to evaluate an application for a new drug by the pharmaceutical company Richardson-Merrell. The drug, being marketed under the name Kevadon, was manufactured by a German company, Chemie Grunenthal. Kevadon had already achieved widespread use in 46 countries throughout the world as a sleep aid and as a cure for morning sickness during pregnancy. Some of the drug's main benefits, according to the manufacturer, were that it was non-addictive, safe for pregnant women, and lacked unpleasant after-effects. Surely, such a beneficial drug would have no trouble sailing through the FDA application process. Kelsey explains, "They gave it to me because they thought it would be an easy one to start on."[3] They were wrong.

Years earlier, while researching various cures for malaria, Kelsey learned that drugs could pass through placental barriers between an unborn child and mother. Reviewing the data on Kevadon, Kelsey felt the absorption and excretion data were inadequate. She also felt that the chronic toxicity studies were too short, the data were too anecdotal, and the controls on the manufacturing process had shortcomings. Thus numerous times she rejected the application.[4]

Richardson-Merrell was anxious to get Kevadon approved. Christmas season, the high season for sales of sleeping pills and sedatives, was fast approaching. The Richardson-Merrell representative was frustrated. He put pressure on Kelsey, making frequent phone calls and numerous personal visits. He even went so far as to complain to Kelsey's bosses that she was being overly stringent and unnecessarily delaying the drug's approval. Nevertheless, despite tremendous pressure from Richardson-Merrell, and despite the fact that the drug had already achieved worldwide popularity, Kelsey remained anchored to her convictions: in her words "I think I always accepted the fact that one was going to get bullied and pressured."

Dr. Kelsey's suspicions about Kevadon proved grimly accurate. First, in December 1960 the *British Medical Journal* published a letter by a physician who had prescribed the drug to his patients. The doctor had noticed an unusually high number of cases of peripheral neuritis (a painful tingling in the feet and arms) among his patients who had taken the drug for an extended period. At the same time, a disturbing phenomenon started to emerge throughout Europe. Babies were being born with severe deformities, including abnormally short limbs, fin-like arms, and toes growing from the hips. Finally, a German pediatrician, Widukind Lenz, discovered that over 50 percent of the mothers with malformed babies had taken the same drug during their first trimester. The culprit? Kevadon—a drug now known more infamously by its unbranded pharmaceutical name, thalidomide.

Because they often defy the strong wishes of others, Right Risks can make us unpopular in the short run. In the long run, however, Right Risks are often rewarded. As a direct result of Dr. Kelsey's efforts, a landmark drug law was approved to strengthen the FDA's control on drug experimentation involving humans. What's more, on August 7, 1962, President John F. Kennedy personally bestowed the highest civilian honor on Dr. Frances Kelsey—the Distinguished Federal Civilian Service award. Forty years later, she was inducted into the National Women's Hall of Fame. However, none of these awards can match the gratification Dr. Kelsey felt from knowing that her resistance to immense pressure ultimately prevented thousands and thousands of deformed babies.

Right Risk: Extraordinary Risks Taken by Ordinary People

In the same way you learn leadership from leaders, law from lawyers, and art from artists, you learn most about risk-taking from risk-takers. Emerson once wrote, "The great distinction between teachers sacred or literary is that one class speaks *from within*, or from experience, as parties and possessors of the fact; and the other class, *from without*, as spectators merely."[5] Throughout the rest of this book, you will read many stories about real life risk-takers, including those from risk's outer edges. However, even the extraordinary examples will be put in service to the ordinary risk-taker.

Lessons from risk's extreme edge can be applied well within its inner fold. Common truths are often most magnified through uncommon feats. Just as courage, composure, and commitment are required of a fighter pilot, so too are they required of the young entrepreneur opening a business, the professor breaking free from the confining prejudices of an academic discipline, and the soldier defying an unjust or immoral order. Courage, composure, and commitment are equally required of the local politician taking a stand on an unpopular issue, the addict reaching out for help (and the jaded cynic reaching back), the young mother leaving the deadly comfort of an abusive relationship, and the volunteer firefighter running into a burning house. Right Risk happens everyday, everywhere.

The promise woven into all Right Risks is our own relevancy. Each of us wants to feel that we have lived a life that matters. We want to make a difference, for ourselves, for our families, for our communities, and for our world. When the choices we make, and the actions we take, are reflections of our higher self, we are ennobled with the knowledge that our life has been worthwhile, at least to ourselves. In the end, the only person we will spend our entire life with is ourselves. We are a lot easier to live with when we are proud of who we are. And we are most proud of ourselves when we take Right Risks.

Questions to consider:

- Describe what attracts you about your big risk. How will facing this risk help you develop and grow as a person?

- Describe what repels you about this risk. What personal fear or inadequacy might it mean facing?

- In what areas of your life do you tend to take more risks (i.e., physical, intellectual, interpersonal, or emotional)? How might you be able to "borrow" from this area in order to take more risks in the areas of your life where you tend to avoid risk?

- Review the four main criteria for a Right Risk—passion, purpose, principle, and prerogative. Based on these criteria, do you think your risk is a Right Risk, or something else?

- Take out a piece of paper and draw a line down the middle of the page. On the left, list some risks that turned out well. On the right, list the risks that turned out badly. Place check marks next to the risks on either column that met the criteria of having been Right Risks. Of those checked, which, if any, do you regret having taken?

Part Two

Readying For The Risk

A high diver does not simply climb up and hurl himself off a 100-foot ladder without a great deal of preparation. Likewise, when facing a giant leap in your own life, there are steps you can take before pursuing your risk. The principles introduced in this part will help you get ready for your big risk.

The first principle, *Find Your Golden Silence,* will help you bring greater focus and intention to your risk. Just because the world seems to be spinning out of control doesn't mean you have to be.

Risk-taking is hard work. The second principle, *Defy Inertia,* will help you overcome the natural inclination to avoid the physical and mental exertion that a challenging risk often demands. Specific inertia-defying techniques are provided.

Sometimes the only thing holding us back in the present are the chiding voices from our past. Principle 3, *Write Your Risk Scripts,* will help you understand, and deal with, the effects of negative self-talk.

Principle 4, *Turn On the Risk Pressure,* talks about some of the mechanisms that you can put in place to help nudge you off your risk platform.

Find Your Golden Silence

"Pure and still, one can put things right everywhere under heaven."

—Lao Tzu, Tao Te Ching

"In the attitude of silence the soul finds the path in a clearer light, and what is elusive and deceptive resolves itself into crystal clearness."

—Mahatma Gandhi

"Silence is golden until it screams right through your bones."

—John Prine, "Storm Windows"

It might seem strange that the first of ten Right Risk principles deals with silence. *Come on,* you might be thinking, *let's fast-forward to where the action is!* Risk-taking is all about action, right? Risk-taking is James Bond throttling a motorcycle off a cliff and parachuting into a waiting speedboat; it's Indiana Jones creeping into a cobwebbed chamber clutching his bullwhip; it's John Rambo demolishing a foreign army all by himself; and it's Lara Croft karate-chopping a baldheaded villain. Risk-taking is, archetypically, the hero putting his life on the line to save the damsel in distress from the racing locomotive. Heck, even risk-taking of a less action-packed nature involves *doing* something. Risk-taking is the protester *marching,* the rebel *resisting,* the entrepreneur *innovating,* the explorer *discovering,* and the writer *opinionating.* Surely risk-taking, that glorious act of courageous audacity, hasn't got anything to do with silence.

True, risk-taking involves action. But before you can *act* you need to *know* what to act on. The reason silence is so important to risk-taking—and in particular Right Risk-taking—is that it helps make your risks more deliberate, intentional, and directed. Silence, extended to the point of mental stillness, has a leveling effect on your perspective, sharpening your powers of discernment. Through silence you become more attuned to your most deeply held beliefs and values, helping you perceive what risks are most compatible with your inner constitution and thus which are truly worth taking. Through silence you can more accurately answer your Right Risk question, *Is this the Right Risk for me?* Hence, the first principle of Right Risk is *find your golden silence.*

There's Gold Inside of You!

Right Risk-taking is about purposeful action: matching the best of your intentions with the best of your behaviors. For your risk to be full of purpose, it has to be anchored to an ideal or a cause that you believe to be worthwhile. But to manifest your convictions through risk, you must first know what you stand for and what you stand against. Silence is the mechanism we use to access our deeper level awareness—our inner gold. When your Right Risk answers emanate from the center of yourself, versus being imposed from the world outside, your conviction is higher and so is your commitment to taking the risk. Let's face it, taking a risk because someone else tells you to is much less fulfilling than taking it of your own initiative. Silence is how we listen to ourselves. For this reason, when readying for your risk it is helpful to follow this dictum: *Careful reflection should precede purposeful action.*

Receptive Silence

Henry David Thoreau, who after spending a year and a half in quiet solitude at Walden Pond certainly earned the right to expound on silence, talks about the necessity to "shake off the village" as a means of connecting to your inner wisdom. Thoreau also underscored the importance of having a sacred place, or what he referred to as a *sanctum sanctorum*. The sanctity of silence is essential in helping the Right Risk-taker to stand apart from the world in order to make sense of it. Ultimately the choice of whether to take a risk resides solely with you and no one else. While the opinions of others should be taken into consideration, you are the one who has to be most comfortable with your risk decision. Having a "sacred place" will help you shut out the world long enough to compare, contrast, and perhaps integrate your own opinions about the risk with the opinions of others. Though the actual location of your sacred space should be picked by you, I find such places as an empty church, peaceful garden, and local library, luxuriously silent

In his wonderfully insightful book *The Courage to Create*, Rollo May writes about the "constructive use of solitude."[1] Like Thoreau, May advises that we periodically disengage from the world and let solitude work for us and in us. Silence helps us relax so that insights and intuitions can break through. The constructive use of solitude is not passive silence but *receptive* silence. We see this receptivity in the artist waiting for inspiration, the writer staring out the window, and the athlete focusing before the contest. It is the attentive silence of listening, not just for words, but also for indications from our intuition about the actions we should take.

Silence takes discipline because it requires being alone, something that seems increasingly difficult for people to do. Yet the rewards for doing so are clear. In silence we strengthen the connection to our inner wisdom, heighten our awareness, and become more exacting in our decision-making. Silence helps us become more clearheaded about what we need to do and why we need to do it. When we sit with silence long enough, we begin to hear and decipher the whispers of our soul. Right Risk-takers use silence to access the wealth—the "gold"—that resides inside them.

Never Stand Still: Perverse Thinking

In the mid 1990s, a regional communications company launched a billboard advertising campaign that implored people to "Never Stand Still!" The underlying message was that to be successful, you must be perpetually on the go. God forbid you be still! Stillness is for weaklings and has-beens; the new breed of winners are those who are furiously busy and fully accessible. The ad was essentially saying, *If you want to avoid missing out on emerging opportunities, you've got to be continually refreshed with up-to-date information, you need "all the news all the time," you've got to be electronically connected! You'll be eminently productive to the extent that you are permanently interruptible.*

"Never Stand Still" is asinine advice. And it is dangerous too. If you are never still, you'll never access your golden silence, and your risks will be taken in a haze of distraction. Instead, standing still is *exactly* what we need to do before taking a major risk. Standing still teaches us composure and poise. Stillness helps focus the risk-taker, enabling her to regulate her emotions and discern the right course of action.

The importance of stillness was well described by Oprah

Winfrey in an editorial in *O Magazine*. In running her production company, *Harpo*, Oprah is pulled in many different directions by many different people. To get centered, she walks into her closet, sits on the floor, and—in her words—"goes still as a stone." She writes, "When I walk out, I am centered on what's most important and can make decisions based on what's right for me—not on what everyone else wants or needs. I've learned that the more stressful and chaotic things are on the outside, the calmer you need to be on the inside."[2]

The French mathematician Blaise Pascal famously said that all of man's problems stem from being unable to sit alone quietly in a room. Those words are more relevant today than they were in his time. We seem to have lost the ability to saunter, to carry on a lingering conversation, to kick back and relax. Instead, anxiety and worry are talked about with pride. With a good deal of self-importance, business people often refer to "what keeps them awake at night," as if stress-induced insomnia were an essential factor in professional success. Busyness has become the defining preoccupation of our age. The only quiet moment we seem to get is that brief interlude in the morning while we are waiting for our computer to boot up. We seem hell-bent on keeping ourselves distracted. We crank up the radio volume in our car, unwind with "comfort TV" at home, cut deals on our cell phone at the playground, and spoon-feed our minds with Internet junk food everywhere we can. We work harder and harder to buy more and more laborsaving devices. And the more we acquire, the unhappier we seem to get (in the U.S., depression is now the leading cause of disability[3]). For as much as our cell phones, pagers, emails, and PDAs have put us in touch with others, they have put us way out of touch with ourselves.

The problem with the boundaryless world is just that—we have no boundaries. We allow the world in with no filter to help us decide the relative importance of each new bit of information. When everything is urgent, all things get trivialized. Again, Thoreau's writing is instructive. He noted that when we fritter back and forth at the whim of the external world, we dull our ability to prioritize what is truly important. In his last book, *Walking,* he writes that this kind of undisciplined thinking results in more than just mental laziness, it can permanently profane how we think so that "all our thoughts shall be tinged with triviality."[4]

The Risk of Silence

Finding your golden silence requires the discipline of setting boundaries. It means unhooking yourself from all the electronic tethers to which you have become accustomed and obliged. It means guarding your private time jealously. It means that an appointment with your silence comes before an appointment with your stockbroker, hairstylist, personal trainer, or plastic surgeon. Finding your golden silence means making your sanity a priority.

In addition to boundary-setting, silence requires courage. Spending time alone carries a tremendous risk: *We might not like our own company.* When we are left alone, we are also left with all our irksome flaws, all our disappointments and regrets, and all our self-condemnation. This is what makes distraction so appealing: it keeps us away from ourselves. When you are flitting back and forth between the TV and Internet, and when you are furiously churning on the productivity treadmill, you don't have to stop and face your own loneliness. As the late spiritual writer and Jesuit priest Anthony de Mello once wrote, "There is an emptiness inside you, isn't there? And when the emptiness surfaces, what do you do? You run away, turn on the television, turn on the radio, read a book, search for human company, seek entertainment, seek distraction. Everybody does that. It is a big business nowadays, an organized industry to distract and entertain us."[5]

While the risks of spending time alone are formidable, the reward is self-assurance. When you persist in silence and allow the discomfort to dissipate—which it eventually will—you wind down the commotion of your inner world and gain peace and clarity. From this posture, with your worries disarmed, your decision-making is more precise and your attitude more confident. Certainly this is a better starting point for taking a risk than a nail-biting anxiety or a spontaneous whimsy.

Shut Up and Go Inside

How do you find your golden silence? By not thinking—literally NOT THINKING. You can't "concentrate" your way into inner silence. Internal silence is about being patient, quelling your inner commotion, and quieting the mind. It is not doing non-auditory things like reading or journaling. Those require too much internal thinking. And inner silence is not prayer, at least not in the traditional sense of reciting words verbally or mentally.

In commenting on how to connect to our inner silence, Franz Kafka once said, "You do not need to leave your room. Remain sitting at your table and listen. Do not even listen, simply wait. Do not even wait, be quite still and solitary. The world will freely offer itself to you to be unmasked, it has no choice, it will roll in ecstasy at your feet."[6] We find our golden silence not through a process of adding to our thoughts but through a process of subtracting from them, or letting them go. While a pure non-thought condition may be biologically impossible (short of unconsciousness), you can get pretty close by letting your thoughts evaporate like mist off a quelling sea until all that is left is stillness. This kind of silence can take literally days to reach, but it is a small investment compared to the dividends it pays in your confidence.

Each year I attend two silent retreats, one in the spring, the other in winter. Not a small feat for an extroverted guy like myself. Though spiritual in nature, these retreats aren't some Kumbaya lovefest. They are rigorously introspective. Each retreat lasts three days and centers on achieving inner and outer silence. While the act of shutting one's mouth is not exceedingly difficult, the act of shutting down one's thoughts is. On the first day of my first retreat, I was struck by how noisy and agitated my mind was. I kept obsessing about all my work obligations—whom I had to call, what I left on my desk, the size of my inbox when I return, etc. But by the end of the second day, my mental treadmill started winding down. Sure, an occasional obsessive thought would float through like a wayward cloud, but the storm had lifted. By the third day I was completely filled with internal stillness and could then begin thinking again in a clear-headed way. The word that best describes this stormless place is "objective." When you sit in silence long enough, your subjective self separates from your objective self. And the more profound the silence, the better able you are to witness your life in an objective way. This out-side-looking-in state is a kind of third-person experience whereby you can look at yourself—with all your flaws—in a way that doesn't incite defensiveness.

Finding your golden silence helps you get ready for your risk by improving your connection to your inner wisdom so that you can "hear" the answers to your higher-order questions *(Who am I trying to become? What is my purpose? What do I want? What risks do I need to take? Where am I playing it too safe? Etc.).* After eight years attending these retreats, I am convinced of the value of silence. Eventually silence becomes so loud that it practically shouts at you with the risks you need to take to further your life. I've come away from each retreat having made a life-changing decision. On two occasions, six years apart, I changed careers. One year I ended up breaking off a relationship that until receiving silence's counsel I didn't have the courage to end. On another occasion, I came to the decision to ask my girlfriend to be my wife (which she did). Now, when readying for a big risk, I wouldn't think of making the decision without consulting my golden silence.

The Wonders of Silence

Considering all the rewards that silence has to offer, it is surprising that more of us don't plug into it. In his terrific book, *Awareness,* Anthony de Mello writes with feigned astonishment, "You mean you understood astronomy and black holes and quasars and you picked up computer science, and you don't know who you are?"[7] De Mello has a good point. We know so much about the outer world while paying very little attention to the inner one. But the inner realm is just as fascinating. Through silence you begin to "know thyself" and come to recognize, trust, and value the wisdom that resides inside you.

Silence is the first principle of Right Risk-taking because it is a first-order risk. Before you can risk on the outside, you must take risks on the inside. You must take the risk of questioning your beliefs and assumptions. You must take the risk of spending time with yourself and face your loneliness. The more frenetic and complicated our world becomes, the more important is silence to help us get centered. Right Risk-taking requires self-assuredness and confidence, both of which gain strength when you have the courage to find your golden silence.

Putting Principle 1 Into Practice

✎ What questions are you grappling with that silence might help you resolve?

_____

_____

✎ How do you handle silence? Is it comfortable or agitated? Do you avoid it? Why?

_____

_____

✎ Do you have a "sacred space"? How often do you go there?

_____

_____

Here are a few things you can do to find your golden silence:

Begin each day with 5 minutes of uninterrupted silence.

Turn off your radio while driving to and from work and enjoy the silence.

Select a "sacred space" and spend time there at least once a month.

Commit to making an annual retreat. Many retreat centers offer retreats that are centered on silence.

Read Thoreau's *Walking*, and then take more sauntering walks.

Stop thinking so much.

Defy Inertia

"The chains of habit are too weak to be felt until they are too strong to be broken."

—Samuel Johnson

"I like the word 'indolence.' It makes my laziness seem classy."

—Bern Williams

Newton's first law of motion, the law of inertia, tells us that a body at rest will remain at rest and a body in motion will stay in motion unless acted upon by an outside force. Inertia is defined as the property of an object to resist changes in its state of motion. We, too, are subject to the laws of inertia. We, too, are bodies at rest or in motion. And inertia inhibits our ability to take risks because it resists our ability to change. Risk-taking is about starting something new or stopping something we've grown comfortable with. In the human law of inertia, risk-taking is the force that shoves us out of our routine or comfort zone. To risk means to change, and because risk-taking causes the usual discomfort that accompanies change, inertia—the cozy comfort of the status quo—is often a more attractive choice. To overcome its debilitating effects, and to help ready yourself for the risk, Right Risk-takers need to learn to *defy inertia*.

Risk-taking as a Vehicle of Change

Through risk-taking we move beyond the comfort of our current condition and overcome inertia. Sometimes this movement is taken through physical action, such as leaving the safety of the ground to scale the face of El Capitan. Other times the movement entails more of a cerebral shift, converting to a new political or religious belief system, for example. Whether physical or intellectual, risk is a vehicle that moves us from *where we are* to *where we want to be*, and you simply can't get from here to there without movement. As a general rule, the greater the distance between your current reality (here) and the destination to which the risk will carry you (there), the more substantial the risk. And the hard truth is, the bigger the gap between *here* and *there*, the more energy, discomfort, and sacrifice will be required to overcome inertia and take the risk. Risk-taking is hard work.

As the path of change, risk-taking is the hard way out of

our current circumstances, the way of initiative. Unfortunately, there is an inverse relationship between initiative and enormity. Thus, the more daunting the risk, the harder it is to muster up the energy to face the challenge, and the easier it is to opt out. We feel dwarfed by the risk's bigness and we think we simply don't have the physical or intellectual wherewithal for the undertaking. For example, many people have shied away from starting their own business not because of the financial commitment, but because they were convinced that the volume of paperwork would be too vexing.

While turning away from the hard work of a large risk is understandable, turning away from small risks makes less sense. In these instances, the reluctance to risk is a function of habit—the behavioral expression of inertia. I see this a lot in my executive coaching practice, where even the smallest risks (in the form of behavioral change) are often met with resistance. For example, I once coached a highly successful, but plateaued, senior executive who, to the annoyance of both his wife and his employees, meticulously planned every waking moment of his life. He knew his rigidity was becoming more than a barrier to career progress, it was hampering his ability to enjoy life as well. More than one person had told him he needed to "lighten up." After he related all the ways in which his overly structured behavior was blocking his personal and professional growth, we began brainstorming how he could increase the amount of spontaneity in his life. Seeing the need to start slow, I made a simple suggestion that on the weekends he begin taking off his wristwatch so that he could allow himself to be unrestricted by time and could begin experimenting with living less rigidly. Meeting my suggestion with a mixture of shock and characteristic rigidity, he replied, "Good God, I could never do that!"

Laziness

It is easy to mistake behavioral inertia with laziness. But laziness isn't about avoiding change, it is about avoiding effort. Ben Franklin called laziness "needless ease," and others have referred to it as *resting before you're tired.* Laziness is different from inertia. Whereas inertia is about resisting changes to our circumstances, laziness is about willful neglect. The plateaued executive wasn't being lazy in resisting the idea of spending a watch-less weekend, he was protecting the status quo of his current condition; he was being habitual.

While laziness and inertia are different, some similarities blur the distinctions between them. Both are concerned with the preservation of the status quo (inertia sits on its habit, laziness sits on the couch). Both resist discomfort. And both respond negatively to risk — inertia resisting the changes that risk will bring, laziness avoiding the effort risk will require. Perhaps the best way to distinguish between the two is to consider how each is overcome. Overcoming inertia requires getting off your habit. Overcoming laziness requires getting off your ass. And both are overcome by taking a risk.

Workaholism: Laziness in Action

Some of the laziest people I know are workaholics. I mean real, honest-to-goodness, 18-hour day, working on the weekend, *dang-I-missed-the-kids-soccer-game-again* workaholics. I've worked with a lot of them in my executive coaching practice. The telltale sign of overwork always indicates to me that the workaholic is being lazy about some part of his or her life. Workaholism is a deceptive form of self-avoidance, of escapism. Some people use work as an excuse to avoid a loveless marriage, others to escape unhappiness with themselves, and some use their job roles as a substitute for an authentic identity. But in each case, the workaholic is using an overabundance of effort in one part of his life while depriving another part that may need it more. In this way, workaholism is about self-neglect.

The neglectfulness of workaholism comes at a price. I have worked with dedicated workers who, other than work, had no real life at all. People whose hard work had paid off in the form of multimillion-dollar salaries, but whose lives were entirely unenviable. People with huge houses, but empty homes. People on their third marriages, with a wake of ruined relationships behind them. People who, aside from their job title, had no identity at all. People who, in real ways, had exchanged portions of their soul for career success. People who, sadly and ironically, make the fatal mistake of spending their whole life . . . making a living.

The saddest thing about workaholics is that nearly all of them have a secret dream that they've squelched. Most often, the dream has nothing to do with their work skill but has everything to do with their passion. I worked with an IT professional who spent absurd hours stringing together lines of software code when his real desire was to do missionary work. He honestly believed that if he just worked hard enough, he would be able to afford to take the risk of living out his passions. But as he churned and churned in a passionless career, his dreams languished. Workaholism brings about the saddest form of personal neglect: dream deprivation.

Too many people trick themselves into believing that being busy equates with personal progress. But a person can be furiously active and entirely stuck. This is what I define as the paradoxical condition of *paralysis in motion*. Like someone running in place, paralysis in motion is an active, but ultimately progress-free, and even regressive, condition. Paralysis in motion is inertia in action, and falling victim to it means we are going nowhere fast.

Defying Inertia

Right Risk-taking requires being alert to the effects of inertia in all its active and inactive forms. Our really big risks, and most especially our Right Risks, require inertia-defying exertion. They require pulling up the roots of our habits, putting down the television remote, and springing into action. How? Here are a few things that you can do to defy inertia:

- **Anchor Your Risk To Your Passion:** It is easier to move into action when we enjoy what we're doing. When the risks you take are anchored to the things you feel most passionate about, you have much more energy and vigor. So ask yourself, "What am I most passionate about?"

- **Play a New Station . . . WIIDR:** Most people have seen the acronym WIIFM, which stands for What's In It For Me? But overcoming inertia requires more than the pull of self-interest. It requires the push of personal accountability. Risk-takers need to tune in to a new station WIIDR, or What If I Don't Risk? Very often when we focus on this question, we realize that not taking a risk is, in fact, a risk! It's the risk of regression.

- **Feed Your Dreams:** Risk-taking is the main way we convert our dreams to reality. No risks, no dreams. Feeding your dream helps you give it gravity, pulling you away from the effects of inertia. Say, like one of my former coachees, you're a senior finance executive, but your dream is to open a shoe store. Instead of listing all the reasons why the risk is unfeasible, conduct some due diligence. Study the industry, go visit a bunch of shoe stores, talk to store owners, join associations, visit with the Small Business Administration, etc. The more you nourish your dreams, the more feasible and real they get. After a while, you'll become so mentally involved in your new world that your physical world will catch up with you. Before you know it, you'll be slapping shoes on stinky feet!

- **Visualize:** Visualization is a mental rehearsal, and it is just as important, if not more so, than rehearsals of a physical nature. The reason is that you rarely (if ever) will have a perfect physical practice, but a visualized rehearsal can be done flawlessly. Fill your mental imagery with as much multisensory detail as possible. In getting ready for a major diving competition, for example, I would picture myself walking on the pool deck and smelling the chlorine; I'd feel the rough sandpaper finish of the diving board under my feet; I'd hear the spray of the water jets pelting the water; and I'd see the aqua-colored diving board and the blue water beyond. Then I would rehearse each dive in slow motion, performing each one with perfection. Your risk images, too, must be as vivid as possible in order for you to begin shifting your risk dreams from pure fantasy to tangible reality.

- **Get a Coach:** The main value a coach brings is fore-thought. Coaches should be able to see the future. The coach's forethought encompasses both farsightedness and shortsightedness—a good coach continuously upholds your ultimate risk destination while simultaneously shining a light on the next step you need to take to sustain your momentum. Along with holding you accountable to your potential, the coach's job is to help you overcome inertia by transporting you from where you are to where you are going. Indeed, the word *coach* still retains its original definition as a carriage (as in *coach* and *carriage*) that takes people from one place to another.

- **Do Your Lead-Ups:** Lead-ups are mini-rehearsals that physically simulate the risk you want to take. Divers, for example, often rehearse new dives on the trampoline. The idea is to help the body build "muscle memory" so that when they attempt the dive "for real," their body will remember what to do. A risk-culminating moment is like the opening night of a Broadway play: When the curtain opens you'll want to make sure that you've had multiple dress rehearsals. The more lead-ups you do, the more confident you'll be and the less likely you'll freak out during the actual risk performance. Lead-ups help us overcome inertia by breaking the risk down in to smaller, more achievable, chunks. Examples of lead-ups include running smaller distances before a marathon, practicing a speech in front of a mirror, role playing with a mentor about how to handle an interpersonal confrontation.

- **Create Desperation:** Sometimes the best thing you can do to overcome inertia is to inject your life with a little desperation. This is the "sink or swim" approach where you plunge ahead, consequences be damned. Desperation stirs things up and forces you to do what is necessary to survive. Quitting one's job before having secured another is a good example.

- **Get Comfortable with the Uncomfortable:** Defying inertia requires moving beyond our comfort zone. Most feelings of discomfort result from loss of control. Since you won't be able to control all the outcomes after taking your big risk, it is a good idea to learn how to deal with this uncomfortable feeling. Here's a fun idea for losing control in a controlled way. After agreeing on a stop signal (such as the right to cry "uncle"), lie back on the floor and let your significant other tickle you for longer and longer durations.

Are You Contending?

An old maxim says the best way to be nothing is to do nothing. A lot of people prefer bragging how they could have been a contender to actually contending. For some, there is a strange comfort in knowing that *they could have* even though *they didn't*. While asserting your potential is much easier than actually living up to it, living in the shadow of your unused potential can be a dreadful burden. Both inertia and laziness leave scars of safety. Many a bar stool has been warmed by the seat of a man whose most taunting recollections are of the risks he didn't take.

Putting Principle 2 Into Practice

 Is your big risk about starting something new or ending something you've grown comfortable with? How might the effects of inertia be impacting your risk?

_____

_____

🖐 How far is the gap between where you want to get to and where you are? How enormous is this risk?

_____

_____

🖐 Based on your answer, how much energy will be required to take your risk?

_____

_____

🖐 How has laziness or busyness impacted your risk? In what ways have you been neglectful of your dreams?

_____

_____

🖐 Refer to the suggestions for defying inertia. How is the risk anchored to your passion?

_____

_____

🖐 How do you plan to "feed the dream"?

_____

_____

🖐 Have you visualized the outcomes yet?

_____

_____

🖐 Who can help coach you through your risk?

_____

_____

🖐 What "lead-up" rehearsals do you need to do?

_____

_____

🖐 In what way is this risk an act of desperation?

_____

_____

🖐 What small things can you do to increase your comfort
with discomfort?

_____

_____

Write Your Risk Scripts

"There is no absurdity so palpable but that it may be firmly planted in the human head if you only begin to inculcate it before the age of five, by constantly repeating it with an air of great solemnity."

—Arthur Schopenhauer

As they exited the aqua-theater, one of the most frequent compliments the audience gave us divers was that we "made it look easy." While easy may have been the result, the word doesn't adequately account for all the rehearsing and fine tuning needed to make the show appear that way. The diving show was extremely well choreographed. Though the audience didn't know it, each dive, each moment on stage, and each bow of gratitude for the audience's applause, was exhaustively rehearsed. Even our smiles were rehearsed! With our index finger, we'd swipe off the saliva from our top teeth, and tuck the upper lip against the whites of our teeth. From the audience it looked like we were smiling, but if you were on the stage with us you'd swear that we had had our top lips removed.

To further enhance the easy look of our performance, both the divers and the announcer regimentally followed a tightly defined script. Scripting was especially important during the comedy portion of the show because we had to dupe the audience for the comedy routine to work. This vaudevillian trickery involved the announcer, one diver as a "straightman," and another diver planted as an unruly audience member. Here is how the setup was choreographed:

ANNOUNCER: Ladies and Gentlemen, before moving on to the next portion of our show, we have a special treat for you. As you can see, one of the divers is warming up on the springboard. Our diver, John, has agreed to perform the dangerous *spotter 3½*. John will do a forward approach and then spring into a reverse somersault, landing *back onto the board* before thrusting himself back in the air to perform 3½ forward somersaults. John is one of only 3 people in the entire world who can perform this dive. As you can imagine, this is an extremely dangerous dive. John will need absolute silence in order to concentrate. Now everyone, silence please.

Getting 2000 audience members to sit still is no easy task. The announcer's sober demeanor was critical to captivating the audience's attention and to creating a sense of believability. Once a hush fell over the unsuspecting audience, the diver would slowly begin his forward approach. Just as he began to hurtle into the air, our plant would blurt out from the middle of the audience, "Hey Jerry, come quick! One of them divers is gonna do a screaming belly whomper!" With that the startled audience would angrily redirect their attention to the audacious derelict. The angrier the audience was, the better the announcer and straightman had set up the comedy routine. More than one comedian got doused with a super-sized cola from an angry patron.

The routine would culminate with the comedian elbowing his way up onto the stage to challenge the straightman to a diving contest. By the time the audience realized they had been duped, they were fully enjoying the ensuing antics. The key to this deception was that it had to seem real. The script was written so as to pull the unwitting audience into the scene so that when they realized the playful deception, they would have fun. Deviating from the script left you in danger of making the audience feel foolish or made fun of. The routine was written so that they felt as if they were in on the joke, not the joke's butt end. To ensure this outcome, as the show's captains, we constantly had to remind our rookie divers to "stick to the script."

Not all high divers were allowed to do the comedy act. And of the ones who were, the best comedians were those who would use the script as a broad framework versus canon law. But a diver could only reach this comedic maturity after performing hundreds of shows as a script loyalist. The first evidence that the diver was maturing as a comedian would be when he would follow the script verbatim but perform it as different characters, each plausibly resembling an actual audience member. One show he might perform the script as a Brooklyn cabby, the next as a nerd, or redneck, or effeminate hairdresser from the local salon. Later, the comedian might try a new facial gesture or tweak a line to discover untapped regions of the audience's funny bone.

With our most seasoned comedians, the routine resembled improvisational theater and was performed with spirited spontaneity. In these instances the script was a point of departure, a launching pad the comedian would use to reach higher levels of comedic communion with the audience. In other words, how the script was used became a barometer of the diver's maturation as a professional. During a diver's first two or three seasons sticking to the script allowed the diver to gain the confidence and experience to take on greater comedic risk later in their careers. Whereas strict adherence to the script was needed to direct a rookie's every move, the more seasoned professional would use it as a baseline, sometimes deviating from it, other times allowing themselves to be directed by it. For the rookie, the script brought standardization and consistency, for the veteran it was a springboard to innovation and experimentation.

Parental Scripting: Echoes From the Past

Our diving-show script provides a useful model for modifying the scripts in our own lives, particularly when it comes to risk. Consciously or unconsciously, unseen scripts direct each of us. By sticking to our scripts, we make life appear predictable and controllable, and therefore safe. This is true regardless of how outdated, or even how unhealthy, our scripts are. A young boy's parents, for example, may compare him to his high-achieving brother. In loving tones, they may say seemingly innocuous things like, "Why don't you go out for the football team like Bobby? Look how successful it has made him." The subtle message construed by the younger sibling is that Bobby is successful and he is not. Even more subtle is the message that the parents want the younger child to be like the older brother, that he is inadequate the way he is, and that he is "less than."

Recognize that in this example there is a huge disconnect between the parent's intent (for the child to be more) and the child's interpretation (that he is less). As the child carries the script into adulthood, and the script nestles itself deeper into his psyche, he begins playing the "less than" role according to script. The older son goes to a prestigious university, the younger to a local community college. The older launches a successful career, the younger can't hold a steady job. The older is responsible, conscientious, and healthy. The younger is unreliable, selfish, and personally neglectful. Following the family scripts, the older son has become more than his parents had hoped for while the younger has been a constant disappointment. An entrenched "less than" script can even lead to such things as substance abuse, financial woes, a string of failed relationships, and anything else you'd expect from people who are "lesser off."

My words shouldn't be interpreted as an indictment of parental scripting. Scripting is an essential form of behavioral conditioning that during our formative years is critical to both our survival and acceptance into the human community. Scripts provide needed parameters for children by acting as mental safety rails that regulate behavior and decision-making. By telling children "don't swim after eating," "don't play with matches," "don't talk to strangers," and "don't get too close to the edge," we teach them the value of safety and cautiousness. But we also teach them to fear taking risks.

Because of their habit-forming influence on human behavior, and because habits restrict our freedom by letting us choose only what is known or familiar, scripts can be a potent form of risk inhibition. That is not to say that a person living a scripted life takes no risks, but that scripts inhibit one of life's most important risks, the risk of freely deciding your own identity, of living a life of your own design.

The problem with scripts is that over time they form mental grooves that channel all our thoughts and actions, directing them like lemmings toward the same outcomes. Over time we simply become more elaborate versions of our earlier selves. The good child progresses into a "goodie two shoes," who becomes a pretentious teenager, who becomes a sanctimonious choir director incapable of facing his or her imperfections, who becomes a shriveled up old prune who—following the "good child" script—never risked enjoying the decadent pleasure of an occasional surrender to all of life's wonderful bad. When we are simply the sum of all our yesterdays, our todays lose the joy of spontaneity and experimentation. Life itself becomes a destiny of predetermined outcomes over which we have relinquished control. Entrenched scripts ultimately lead to cognitive imprisonment—a life void of free choices.

As we mature into adulthood, our scripts may not keep pace with the demands of an adult life. When our behaviors and decisions are dictated by outdated scripts, we become puppets to the past, responding like well-behaved children to complex situations that require a higher degree of maturity and a lower degree of restraint. A more useful and beneficial approach would be to mimic the diving comedians by doing improvisational riffs on our core risk scripts.

Build On Your Risk Scripts

A lot has been written in self-help literature about the need to rewrite outdated or unhealthy scripts. While in principle I agree that re-scripting is important, in practice it is extremely difficult to do. Short of intense psychotherapy or a cataclysmic life-changing event (which often precedes therapy), I think that a full re-scripting is next to impossible. However, I do believe that, as in the diving show, our basic scripts can be used as a springboard to higher levels of risk aptitude and personal maturity. Rather than rewrite our scripts entirely, we would be better served to build on our scripts and use them as a source of identity renewal, a starting point on which our identities can mature and progress.

For example, the rock star Madonna is often admired for her ability to "reinvent" herself. But in my opinion, her various identities (boy toy, material girl, erotica vixen, Kabbalah soul woman, etc.) all basically stem from the same script, a script that says, namely, *I am valuable and lovable to the extent that people want me.* Her greatness isn't a function of her ability to re-script herself as much as it is her willingness to use her foundational script as a source of identity exploration. If she were to convert her need to *get* attention into a need to *give* attention, say becoming an aid worker in Somalia, then I would believe that a full re-scripting and identity conversion had taken place.

Identifying the scripts that drive your behavior and understanding how they inhibit you is a critical step in readying yourself for your big risk. Though the basic scripts that people follow are virtually limitless, below are some of the more common ones that I've run across in my executive coaching practice. Keep in mind that when people seek me out for coaching, it is often because they have gotten "stuck" and are searching for ways to get moving again. Thus the nine scripts offered here are limiting scripts, that is, scripts that keep you from progressing toward your risk.

Nine Limiting Scripts

---

❶

"I am not enough"

Consequences
- Consumptive need for self-improvement to compensate for feelings of inadequacy
- Gnawing sense of dissatisfaction and discontent
- Self-berating, perfectionistic
- Constantly proving him/herself to self and others
- Hyper-ambitious

Inhibited Risks
- Risk of self-acceptance
- Risk of *settling down*
- Risk of embracing feelings of incompleteness.

---

❷

"They will like me if I am pretty/handsome"

Consequences
- Preoccupation with outward appearances
- Interpersonally shallow, narcissistic, self-preoccupied
- Worth determined by physical attractiveness
- Slave to fashion

Inhibited Risks
- Risks that threaten one's image or appearance
- Risk of accepting one's ugliness

- Risk of forming deep relationships based on interior attractiveness

---

❸

"The more I produce, the more valuable I am"

Consequences

- Preoccupation with doing, busybody behavior
- Unable to relax, time regimented, and often ill-at-ease
- Lacks spontaneity
- Draws personal worth based on the volume of work accomplished

Inhibited Risks

- Risk of inaction, of *being* versus doing

---

❹

"If I have more than you, I'll be better than you"

Consequences

- Preoccupation with material wealth
- Financial value and personal value equated
- Possessive, stingy, and often elitist

Inhibited Risks

- Risk of generosity, of *giving* versus *getting*
- Risk of judging people according to character versus compensation
- Risk of acknowledging one's inferiority
- Risk of humility

---

❺

"I must always be in control"

Consequences

- Hyper-focus on risk mitigation and catching mistakes
- Lives in constant fear of chaos
- Dominating of others, bossy, dogmatic
- Personal rigidity and lack of spontaneity
- Joyless

Inhibited Risks

- Risk of giving up control and living unattached to outcomes
- Risk of following other people's lead.

"You can't trust anyone; people always let you down"

Consequences

- Unrealistically low expectations of others
- Suspicious, questions the motives of others
- Gravitation toward situations that validate their distrust
- Emotionally distant, frigid, and unable to form lasting relationships
- Lonely

Inhibited Risks

- Risk of putting down emotional guard, chancing rejection
- Risk of obligations associated with deep friendships
- Risk of intimacy, closeness, and commitment.

---

⑦

"They will like me if I am nice (even if I secretly dislike them)"

Consequences

- People pleasing or pandering behavior
- Insincere, inauthentic, and disingenuous
- Self-resentful. Satisfies the needs of others at the expense of meeting one's own needs and wants
- Can become petty and spiteful

Inhibited Risks

- Risk of displeasing others by asserting one's true opinion
- Risk of meeting one's own needs first
- Risk of authenticity, of being one's true self

---

⑧

"I am damaged goods"

Consequences

- Victim mentality, prone to blaming others for one's lot in life
- Resentful of other people's happiness or success
- Self-doubting, self-pitying, and self-sabotaging

- Deep feelings of being misfit, motto: "No one understands me."

Inhibited Risks

- Risk of assuming personal responsibility for one's own station in life.
- Risk of intimacy, closeness, and commitment.

---

⑨

"I am unlovable"

Consequences

- Deep feelings of low self-worth and/or self-loathing
- Successive failed relationships
- Bitter and resentful

Inhibited Risks

- Risk of self-acceptance
- Risk of assuming the obligations and responsibilities of personal fidelity (i.e., self-love).

The Power of Personal Mantras

As part of getting ready for a risk, it is important to keep your scripts from limiting your progress. Though a complete scriptural rewrite may not be possible without extensive soul-searching, working with my coachees has taught me that it is possible to influence them. One way to do this is to pick a personal mantra.

To illustrate how this works, consider the case of Jon, one of my coachees. Jon's actions were directed by the script I see most often in coaching executives, the "I am not enough" script. In Jon's instance, his "not enough" script compelled him to take on huge volumes of work in the hopes of getting promoted to the senior ranks (which he equated with "enough"). I am not talking about going the extra mile, I am talking about taking business calls at the dinner table, working till 2 AM, starting again at 6 AM, working weekends, skipping vacations, etc. Yet for all his hard work, Jon couldn't get promoted. He was like a hot air balloon with a giant hole in the top; try as he might, he could only get so high. The senior executives viewed him as overly eager, which they interpreted not as a wealth of ambition but as a lack of confidence. He was *too* available, *too* accessible, and *too* intense. What would happen, they wondered, if promoting him actually worsened the problem?

After talking about all the ways his "not enough" script had permeated every area of Jon's life—from his constant sense of dissatisfaction to his inability to sit still—he decided to risk assuming a whole new set of behaviors. Instead of rabidly pursuing getting promoted, he decided that he would be better served to focus on developing his confidence. I asked Jon what he would look like if he were "enough." He blurted out reflexively, "I'd stop giving such a shit." After a good laugh, he got more serious. "It is hard to even imagine what 'enough' would look like. I feel so unfinished. But since you asked, I guess when I walked into a room, I'd look *calm* and *confident*." After a brief pause he added, "Like a Cheshire cat after mating season!"

Jon decided that he would adopt *"calm confidence"* as his mantra. Every time he felt himself starting to get all wigged out, he'd take a deep breath and think his magic words. Since Jon had allowed himself to essentially become a 24-hour service station, he also had to learn to set new boundaries, backing up his newfound words with specific actions: no calls during dinner, no 18-hour days, and no skipping vacations.

After a few fits and starts, Jon began noticing real changes, not just in himself, but in how people responded to him. It was odd—the calmer he was in the presence of others, the calmer others became. Moreover, he was now better able to assert his boundaries when people infringed on his time, which built his confidence. We both knew that Jon was making progress when, after an intense business meeting with an upset client, Jon's boss commented, "Thank God you were there, Jon. You were the calmest person in the room."

It is important to note that Jon's mantra didn't "cure" his feelings of being incomplete. How could it? All of us are works in progress. And though his "not enough" script was limiting—particularly to his career—it also served him in some way. It was too closely tied to his ambition to want to discard entirely. Rather, his "calm confidence" mantra offset his feelings of inadequacy, and in this sense made him "enough." By regulating his internal condition through the use of a personal mantra, and by focusing on building his confidence, Jon started to demonstrate the self-assurance that is critical at the senior levels. Thus he has a much more realistic chance of getting promoted now than when he was taking on voluminous amounts of work.

Mantras as Risk Advancers

In readying for our risk, the benefit of a personal mantra is that it helps boost our courage, allowing us to take risks we might otherwise avoid. For example, when I started in my role as an executive coach at Accenture, a prestigious management and technology consulting company, I was so afraid of coaching the company partners that I actually considered forgoing the opportunity. Prior to moving into the role, I was a middle manager and had reported to a few of these execs, so I knew personally how intimidating and level-conscious a few of them could be. Knowing that most of them were older than I only added to my anxiety. Yet, my success as a coach (and their progress as coachees) would be contingent upon my ability to give them unvarnished feedback. Unless I could develop a stronger backbone, I would be utterly useless to them. Coaching is all about demonstrating and instilling courage. What kind of role model would I be if I were a wimpy coach?

About the time I was to move into the role, I came across a poem by Mahatma Gandhi titled *Resolution*. One line in particular resonated with me, "I shall not fear anyone on earth." Until reading the poem, I had always assumed that Gandhi had been fearless in affecting such transformational change. It caught my attention because I knew that for Gandhi to declare this as a resolution for his future, he must have experienced fear of others in his past.

A few days later I happened to watch a documentary on Martin Luther King, Jr. Living in Atlanta, King is one of my heroes, and I never miss a chance to learn about his life. It turns out King was a great admirer of Gandhi and even had a picture of him hanging over the archway to his dining room. King had patterned his principles of nonviolence and passive resistance after Gandhi's. In his last speech, delivered the night before he was assassinated, King talks of the promised land and says, prophetically, that he may not get there with us. Then, as if he were speaking directly to me, he says, "Tonight *I am fearing no man.*" Once again I was struck with the fact that for King to have made a special point that he was fearing no man *on that night* must have meant that he feared men on other occasions.

It was somehow liberating for me to know that the fearful feelings I had about coaching the company bosses were very similar to the ones experienced by King and Gandhi during their struggles against the ruling authorities. Feeling part of a noble lineage, I borrowed the words of both men to come up with a mantra of my own: "I will fear no man." That simple mantra helped me get ready for taking on the new job by stiffening my backbone during those intense moments when I found myself feeling intimidated by my coachees' position or age. My mantra helped me coach more assertively, which, in turn, built my credibility and earned the executives' respect as well.

Keep it Simple

For a personal mantra to be effective, it has to be exquisitely simple, certainly no more than a sentence long. Also, your mantra should compensate for whatever risk-limiting scripts you are operating under at a specific moment in time. Thus don't feel obliged to keep your mantra any longer than is useful to you. Here are some mantras that I've found useful in helping my coachees risk more confidently:

No risk, no reward	Let go	Focus!
No boundaries	Know boundaries	It's all good
Get over yourself!	Insist on yourself!	Keep the faith
Personal fidelity	Stay in the moment	Trust God
One day at a time	Follow your bliss	Carpe Diem

The word *mantra* derives from two Sanskrit words; *manas* ("totality of mind") and *trai* ("to set free from"). Thus the literal translation is "to set free from the mind." Verbal or mental repetition of the mantra is a powerful technique to help you get ready for your risk because it frees you from your more debilitating scripts. As you move closer to your risk, however, you may wish to elaborate on your mantra by doing such things as writing a personal mission statement, or drafting your own "declaration of independence" to explain your philosophies about life (writing this book, for example, is a declaration about my own beliefs). In other words, over time, you may be able to slowly craft new, healthier, scripts to live by.

Putting Principle 3 Into Practice

✎ When facing a big risk, what do you tell yourself with your internal "self-talk"?

_____

_____

✎ Of the nine basic scripts provided in this chapter, which ones, if any, resonate with you? Is there a different script that you seem to follow? If so, try to define it in one sentence.

_____

_____

✎ Once you have identified your basic limiting script, pick a simple catch phrase (i.e., personal mantra) to offset its effect on you.

_____

✎ What types of life changes must you put in place to support your mantra? For example, if your mantra is "personal fidelity," what types of things can you do to demonstrate being faithful to yourself? How will you start recognizing, acknowledging, and honoring your own needs?

_____

_____

Turn on the Risk Pressure

"*Public opinion is a weak tyrant compared with our own private thoughts.*"

—Henry David Thoreau

"*Numerous decent, wholesome young persons permit themselves to become involved in unwholesome pursuits which they do not personally condone or even enjoy, because they are ashamed to say no when the gang says yes.*"

—Martin Luther King, Jr.

The fourth principle in readying for your risk is that you need pressure to nudge yourself from your current situation—your risk platform. Consider again the high dive. The moment preceding the jump is full of tension. The diver is well aware of being watched. The expectant eyes of the audience create pressure—pressure to leap, pressure to perform, pressure not to let the audience down. This is a pressure she's felt before. She's been dealing with it since she was a kid doing belly flops at the local pool. Other folks have pressured her too, like her parents, coach, and friends. But most of all, she's felt pressure from herself. She constantly goads herself to dive higher and perform better.

Our lives have many points of risk pressure that act on us by forming an acute dissatisfaction with our current circumstances. Often our dissatisfaction intensifies until it grabs us by the throat and screams, "Take the risk and jump, you fool!" We reach this leaping point when the risk of changing outweighs the risk of staying the same. For example, when faced with a career transition, the risk decision often boils down to a choice between a known unhappiness and an unknown *possibility* of happiness. We become increasingly dissatisfied with our current job until it becomes nearly impossible to get out of bed and face another day at the office. We may call in sick to avoid the risk decision; but the decision won't let us go. The more we allow ourselves to live in a state of dissatisfaction, the more we feel as if we are living a lie, and the pressure builds. Although many of us have a tremendous capacity for tolerating misery, eventually we will reach our high-dive moment and decide the risk of changing outweighs the risk of staying in a suffocating situation.

The trick in applying risk pressure is to apply enough to help you progress toward your risk, but not so much that it causes you to choke. To turn on your risk pressure means to become increasingly dissatisfied with your current circumstances by creating what I call *purposeful anxiety*. We all know that too much anxiety is unhealthy. But anxiety in lower degrees, and directed toward a purposeful aim, can be evidence of conscientiousness. Purposeful anxiety keeps us alert to the potential dangers and opportunities that the risk may hold. In balanced amounts, it also keeps inertia at bay.

Personal Performance Pressure

Perhaps the strongest risk pressure comes from the demands we place on ourselves. Like the other types of pressure covered in this chapter, it has a good and bad side. At the negative extreme, the pressure we put on ourselves can be debilitating. We tell ourselves, "Good is not good enough. Good is *never* good enough." For example, I once counseled a senior executive who was in a constant state of agitation. The executive was a tremendously gifted professional who had risen through the ranks because of her fine-tuned ability to solve problems and produce stellar business results. By every measure, she was a success. Her sharp business acumen had been handsomely rewarded; her annual salary was well over a million dollars, but that was part of the problem. She drove herself to the point of exhaustion trying to justify her income. The pressure she put on herself was a form of guilt assuagement. *If I can just work hard enough,* she'd think, *I'll deserve this much money.*

In instances like these, the hell-bent pressure to perform teeters dangerously close to self-hatred, where one constantly berates oneself for not being *good enough*. The poison in this kind of thinking is that your motivation for taking a given risk operates out of a desire to "fix yourself." This results in a perverse form of perfectionism that leaves you perpetually dissatisfied because *good enough* is illusory; once you get to *good enough*, you realize that it is *not enough* . . . and you cycle through this grass-is-greener treadmill all over again. Even those risks that are successful leave you perpetually unsatisfied.

But personal performance pressure can be a very effective means of nudging you off your risk platform. For example, one driver of performance pressure is having something to prove. How we apply this pressure is different, depending on whether we are proving something to ourselves or to others. When we are out to prove something to ourselves, we think, *I can do this*. But when we are out to prove it to someone else, we think, *I'll show them* I can do this. This latter pressure is what you might call a positive form of negative motivation. In essence, you are taking the risk because you resent your detractors telling you that you can't. The fact is, sometimes our detractors prompt our most audacious risk behavior. In these situations the most useful type of internal motivation is often good old-fashioned spite.

It was spite, for example, that helped Jake Burton Carpenter invent the sport of snowboarding. In 1977 Carpenter quit his job at a Park Avenue investment firm, moved to Vermont, and began making snowboards in his garage. As with many such risks, he met with early failure, finding himself over $100,000 in debt. Things were so desperate, he even had to move back to New York to tend bar and teach tennis lessons. To the bewilderment of his friends, however, he also persisted with his snowboarding fantasies. Carpenter explains, "Out of spite I kept at it. I had to show my friends that they were wrong." And indeed they were. Now Burton Snowboards is a premier supplier to one of America's fastest growing sports, and Jake Burton Carpenter is considered snowboarding's patron saint.[1] As Carpenter demonstrates, the secret knowledge that we are capable of far more than we are given credit for can fuel our ambition and help us take leaps of faith. Thus one of the best things you can do when readying for your risk is to pinpoint what you are out to prove and to whom you have to prove it.

Intriguingly, sometimes our detractors are purposely saying "you can't" in order to inspire us to say "yes I can!" For example, Ed Catmull, the cofounder and President of Pixar Animation, notes that getting people to prove something is an essential part of the innovation process. Catmull says, ". . . there have been many times when people who work for me have told me that a project was possible, and I'd look at them and say 'I don't think so.' And they'd come back at me with this fervor to explain why they thought I was wrong and why they should go ahead with it. That's precisely when you want to let them go ahead. The very act of doubting them, and then letting them proceed, motivates them to go ahead and prove that they're right."[2]

Peer Pressure

When it comes to risk, few pressures are as powerful and persuasive as peer pressure. At the root of peer pressure is acceptance. We do something risky because we don't want to be seen as uncool—we want people to like us. Giving in to peer pressure is a form of conformity: We want to be included, on the inside, part of the group. Hence many of the risks we take are as a result of the goading taunts of our peers. The first time most fraternity pledges get drunk, for example, their friends are beside them chanting "chug, chug, chug." And while former President Bill Clinton may not have inhaled, a lot of other people did and peer pressure usually had something to do with it. You know the scene: Neil Young's *Heart of Gold* warbling in the background, a group of friends sitting in a circle, the glow of a black light, that pretty girl you've been trying to muster the courage to ask on a date, and suddenly someone passes you a hand-rolled cigarette muttering something that sounds like "eer." Suddenly you feel the daring eyes of everyone in the room—*will he* or *won't he.* This is a high-dive moment!

Like personal performance pressure, peer pressure has many redeeming qualities. It is the pressure of our peers, after all, that gives us the support to try things we otherwise wouldn't have. As fellow high divers, my teammates and I were always cheering each other on to greater heights. We'd stand on the pool deck and cajole, wheedle, and dare each other to try increasingly difficult tricks. I remember, for example, being in Germany and learning a trick called a double half—two somersaults with a half twist. Performing it from a mini-trampoline set atop a 10-meter platform made the trick all the more difficult. Fortunately, prodding me from the pool deck was Steve Schriver. Steve and I had been through a lot together. We had even driven across America in my oft-breaking Fiat Spyder . . . with no radio. As teammates, but also as rivals, Steve and I were always egging each other on. We enjoyed competing against each other because it furthered both of our talents. I trusted Steve. He knew how to play, but he also knew how to focus. So when I decided to learn this new trick, I asked Steve to coach me through it. After a considerable amount of positive, but persistent, pressure from Steve, I was able to do the dive. In that moment, Steve did what I couldn't do for myself: hold me accountable to my potential. The effectiveness of the positive form of peer pressure is one reason why you should enlist a few key peers to keep the pressure on you when readying for the risk.

Pressure of Potential Outcomes

Our attitude toward risk is in large measure a function of how we envision the potential outcome, whether we see the risk as an opportunity for gain or a threat of loss. It was the promise of a huge payoff, for example, that caused so many people to risk their careers by abandoning the familiar terrain of the traditional business world to become Buckaroo Banzais of the dot-com "space." In the worst examples our desire for gain is driven by greed, causing us to take risks in the hopes of becoming more powerful, famous, attractive, and/or wealthy. Charmed by the attraction of gain, people have maxed out credit cards in Vegas, married wealthy but loveless partners, bought huge volumes of stocks on margin, and "cooked the books" at large corporations like Enron and Worldcom.

In the same way the potential gain can pressure us to seek out risk, the potential outcome of loss can pressure us to avert it. Loss looms larger than gain because most of us know from experience that loss is more permanent and more upsetting. Loss prompts painful recollections of past failures, such as career setbacks, financial hardship, and failed relationships—all things we don't care to repeat. For this reason, the threat of loss causes us to clutch, to grab hold of, to keep what's ours. With the stubborn consternation of a 3-year-old, we will hold on to what we've got and say "mine!" For example, a friend was once dating a woman for whom he had lukewarm feelings. After tiring of his indifference, she decided to break up. It was only when faced with the real possibility of losing the woman that my friend suddenly "realized" how much he loved her and started desperately trying to get her back. I am convinced that it wasn't so much that he really loved her; he just hated losing her.

While the pressure associated with the potential outcome of loss most often causes risk aversion, it can also pressure us to take risks. Part of the pressure stems from the feeling that if you don't act fast, you'll miss out. Marketers play into the fear of loss when they threaten consumers with limited-time offers. "Today only!" and "If you act right now, we'll throw in the . . . " are old marketing taglines designed to get you to think, *Uh oh, if I don't act fast I'll lose!*

As illustrated by this story from my college days, our perception of gain or loss, and thus our attitude about the risk, can change instantly. In 1983 I performed in a television commercial for McDonald's. The advertisement, which was pitching their 100% grade A eggs, featured me performing a back one and a half somersault with two and a half twists—which I performed twice in the course of the 30-second spot. The ad ran regionally along the East Coast and was being considered as one of their official Olympic spots for the upcoming L.A. games. It was an exciting time for me; I was on the verge of making a name for myself and getting my 15 minutes of fame.

Like gymnastics and figure skating, diving is a sport where the winner is determined by an accumulation of awarded points. The sport has a sort of upward mobility—the more complex and difficult the dive, the greater the total number of possible points. Most often the diver who performs the repertoire of dives with the highest cumulative degree of difficulty—along with consistency and grace—wins. But at the elite levels, it takes more than difficult dives to prevail, it takes an extra edge. Though numerical scoring helps bring objectivity to the sport, the points the diver receives are awarded through subjective means: human judges. The "edge" the diver searches for often plays to this subjectivity. Before a contest, some divers work the pool deck like politicians, glad-handing the judges in the hopes of winning over their affections. Divers know that it is harder to give a low score to someone you know and like. The diver who has a "name" has a slight subjective edge. In a sport where a contest can be decided by less than a tenth of a point, name matters.

Much to my dismay, just prior to the commercial's national debut, a sports writer from West Virginia University (where I was a student) made a disturbing discovery—by performing in the ad, I had violated an NCAA rule prohibiting amateur athletes from making product endorsements. Though I received no money for making the ad, because I used my talents to promote McDonald's products, it was viewed as a product endorsement. In my zeal to make a name for myself, I had neglected to check into the NCAA rules before signing the contract to do the commercial. The NCAA was now threatening to ban me from competing in intercollegiate athletics altogether. Instead of making a name for myself, I now faced a real possibility of losing my full athletic scholarship, not to mention letting down my parents, team, and myself. I have always been grateful to the McDonald's Corporation for agreeing to pull the ad. I am sure that they lost thousands of dollars in the process.

Aside from sophomoric hubris, this story illustrates how it is possible to ricochet back and forth between the pressure of gain and loss in the same episode. When the sports writer notified me of the rule violation, my attitude shifted instantaneously from *hope for gain* to *fear of loss*. My perception, of course, was based on what I *expected* to happen. Before becoming aware of the NCAA rule violation, I expected that the commercial would bring me a small degree of fame and thus help me win more competitions (gain). After finding out about the violation, I expected that my scholarship would be taken away and that I'd be forced to drop out of school for lack of money (loss). Neither condition was assured, however. It was also possible for the opposite to occur. Pairing me with scrambled eggs, the commercial could very well have made me the laughingstock of the diving world ("Hey, there goes Bill McEgghead!"). At the same time, if the NCAA did take my scholarship away, perhaps McDonald's would have kept the ad and offered me advertising residuals to offset my loss. The point is, the pressure of potential outcomes is driven by our *perception* about what the future may hold. This pressure strikes us most forcefully in our imagination, in what we envision the risk will give us or take away from us.

While I think that both gain and loss can be effective risk pressure systems, there is a danger in framing each in purely material or economic terms. When we do, the predominant principle governing our behavior is greed, which, as demonstrated by the corporate implosions of the early 2000s, makes for notoriously bad decisions. Instead of narrowly framing your risk as "What will it *get* me," I find it more useful to frame it as "Where will it *take* me." In other words, not "How will my bank account grow," but "'How will *I* grow." When you broaden your definition of gain or loss to include qualitative references—like furthering the development of your character—your risk takes on a higher order purpose, and your decision-making becomes more composed than it is when governed solely by greed.

Organizational Pressure

Pressure to take or avoid risks in organizational settings often starts outside of the company. With public companies, for example, shareholders exert incessant pressure for ever-greater profits. Sometimes this pressure can embolden a company to move into new businesses or markets, create new product lines, or develop new technologies. For example, the pressure exerted from bedazzled shareholders caused many steadfast "brick and mortar" companies to create and pursue strategies for moving into the embryonic dot-com space. Other times, however, shareholders can cause companies to be risk averse. For example, shareholder pressure to drive down costs can inhibit a company's ability to invest in opportunities that, though risky, have a significant upside potential. In these instances, funding decisions dictate which strategic initiatives will be pursued, and which won't. Often initiatives that are viewed as most risky—but with the most upside potential—are scrapped first.

Organizations themselves provide pressure that fosters or inhibits risk-taking behavior. Performance management and appraisal systems are two examples. As the saying goes, *you get what you measure.* If employees are held accountable to high sales quotas, they will feel a pressure to produce sales. If managers are held accountable for low employee turnover, they'll feel pressure to retain their people. If the annual review process involves assessing and rewarding employees based on their number of innovative product ideas, they'll feel pressure to be creative. But organizational pressure points can also lead to dysfunctional workforce behavior. As a consultant, I once worked for a utility company whose market had become increasingly deregulated. Its employees, who had grown up with the stability of government regulation, were uncomfortable in dealing with a far less predictable environment. While the company was battling with a sharp increase in unregulated competition, its employees had grown apathetic and were unresponsive to executive pleas for urgency.

After struggling with how to transform the workforce from order-takers to risk-takers, senior management decided to leak word of an "at risk list"—a list of all the employees who were in danger of losing their jobs. Though no employee ever actually saw the list, the message was clear: ratchet up production or get out. Though this type of "hold-a-gun-to-their-heads" strategy worked in the short run, over the long haul it resulted in a great deal of cynicism. Fear-based pressure tactics to increase risk-taking behavior among employees are unsustainable and nearly always end in bitterness and resentment. Nevertheless, in the short run, sometimes the only way to prod people off their risk platform is to make it riskier for them *not* to jump.[3]

Risk's Perfect Storm

As mentioned earlier, the trick is to apply pressure in a measured way. Too much pressure, like too much ambition, can cause a person to crack. There is a point at which the anxiety that pressure creates isn't purposeful at all. There is a point at which anxiety turns into plain old desperation, and the more desperate our situation becomes, the wilder our behavior gets. Consider the true story of how a lone risk-taker helped bring down a 232-year-old British banking institution, momentarily threatening the entire British banking system. The story is so astonishing that it was later made into a feature film staring a famous *Star Wars* movie star (I'll divulge who at the story's end). It is a cautionary tale of what can happen when intense risk pressures—brought on by ourselves, our peers, our perception of loss and gain, and our organizations—converge together. It is the story of risk's perfect storm.

Established in 1763, Barings Bank was Britain's first merchant bank. Within 20 years of the bank's inception, its founder, Francis Baring, became so powerful that he was elected to the British parliament and made a baronet. Before long, Barings Bank was conducting financial transactions throughout the world and had earned the notable distinction of being the bank of the royal family. Former Princess Diana was herself a great-granddaughter of a Baring. Over the course of its rich and varied history, Barings helped finance the Napoleonic wars and America's Louisiana Purchase.

Enter Nick Leeson.

Barings hired Nick Leeson as a back office clerk in 1989. Early in his career he was sent to Jakarta to clean up the operations of the bank's Indonesian back office. Leeson proved to be a deft manager, and based on this early success was sent to improve the similar operations of other fledgling Far East and European outposts. Then in 1992 Leeson was asked to manage Barings' Singapore operations. But because of staffing shortages, he was put in charge of both futures trading and back-office record keeping. This was a highly unusual move and one fraught with inherent conflicts of interest, the danger being that if trading losses were incurred, there would be a tremendous temptation to manipulate the back-office accounting records. This excessive concentration of powers was not lost on Leeson, who in his aptly titled autobiography, *Rogue Trader: How I Brought Down Barings Bank and Shook the Financial World*, commented, "I was in a bizarre situation . . . I could see the whole picture, and it was so easy. I was probably the only person in the world to be able to operate on both sides of the balance sheet."[4]

To Barings' great misfortune, Leeson could not resist the temptation.

At first, Leeson's story is a tale of wanton greed, both his and Barings. He talks lustfully about how when he first stepped onto the trading floor he could "smell and see the money." Later he says, "We were all driven by profits, profits, and more profits . . . I was the rising star." But as the story progresses, the pressure driving Leeson the most became the threat of loss. An early mistake would snowball into one of the greatest acts of corporate malfeasance of all time.

It all started when one of Leeson's new trading recruits made an honest but expensive error. Futures trading involves an open outcry communication method whereby a trader from one company yells his offer to buy or sell to a trader from another company, who yells back whether they accept or reject the offer. To aid in communicating, traders often use coded hand signals, similar to the messages sent back and forth between the pitcher and the catcher in baseball. It is an error-prone process, and amidst the trading floor chaos, Leeson's new recruit mistakenly sold 20 futures contracts when her client had signaled her to buy. This mistake, which was discovered at the end of the trading day, amounted to £20,000. Knowing that the recruit would likely be fired if her mistake was discovered by Leeson's superiors, and being frustrated with Barings because "the mean tight-fisted bastards" wouldn't let him hire someone more experienced, Leeson decided to bury the mistake in a dormant back-office error account that had been set up some time earlier. Her mistake had now become his problem . . . and crime.

Loss has a strange effect on people, often causing two extremely different reactions. The *once bitten* effect is what happens when you become overly cautious in the present because of recollections of painful losses in the past. The *double or nothing* effect occurs when in an effort to recoup losses you take on even greater risk. Such was the case with Leeson. Within three days, the initial losses had tripled to £60,000. He recounts, "I was determined to win back the losses. . . . I traded harder and harder, risking more and more." Later he states, "I had to take unprotected risks to try to win back the lost money. And although I was winning sometimes, more often I was losing."

Unfortunately, Leeson was betting on an unstable Asian market, and the market only got worse. With his losses swelling, he knew that getting caught would mean more than the loss of the new recruit's job, it would mean the loss of his as well. Thus in an effort to win the lost money back, Leeson began taking on even greater risk, and continued hiding the losses in the error account. By the end of 1993, though Leeson's accounting showed that he had made £10 million (accounting for a full 10% of all of Barings' profits), in reality he was hiding losses totaling £23 million! Based on the false profits Leeson was reporting, the unsuspecting Barings awarded Leeson a bonus of £135,000. Convinced they had a real whiz-kid on their hands, and wanting to keep the profits rolling, Barings provided Leeson with a company financed apartment and sponsored his membership to Singapore's exclusive Cricket Club.

Meanwhile, Leeson's reputation as the kid with a golden touch grew. To his peers, Leeson was becoming a powerbroker, someone to be reckoned with. Leeson notes, "To the outsider, I looked like Nick Leeson, the trading superstar who moved the Nikkei this way and that, the gambler with the biggest balls in town." But the truth was far less glamorous: again in his own words, "I was drowning like an insect stuck in resin, clawing hopelessly but unable to pull myself out."

As a result of Leeson's criminal charade, Barings' confidence in Leeson increased, and they entrusted him with more and more money throughout 1994. But unbeknownst to anyone but Leeson, his error account was nearly hemorrhaging. Driven by a downturn in the Asian markets and exacerbated by the economic impact of an earthquake in Kobe, Japan, Leeson's hidden losses swelled to a staggering £208 million. To continue his frenetic gambles, Leeson requested—and received—more and more capital from the home office. To convince the home office that the large amounts of capital it was sending were not at risk, Leeson forged records to show that big payments were due from prominent clients.

Finally, as a result of an internal audit, Barings became suspicious, so much so that a few senior executives decided to fly to Singapore to question Leeson about his large capital outlays. But on February 23, 1995, before Barings could meet with Leeson, he quietly slipped out of the office, leaving a handwritten note that said, "I'm sorry." He would be caught a few days later while trying to sneak back to England. When Barings finally tallied Leeson's wreckage, it was too late to save the bank. He had racked up losses in excess of £660 million—or the equivalent of over $1.4 *billion* U.S. dollars! With its debt far exceeding its liquidity, and with the British banking system under a real threat of collapse, the Dutch financing group ING agreed to purchase the 232-year-old institution for the paltry sum of £1.[5]

And as for Leeson? After serving 3½ years of a 6½ year sentence in a Singaporean jail for fraud and forgery, his sentence was commuted for good behavior. But don't envy Mr. Leeson. He has had his share of misfortune. His wife divorced him during his incarceration. To make matters worse, he was diagnosed with colon cancer. And though Leeson has become a sought-after professional speaker, fetching up to $100,000 per speech, the British government garnishes 70% of his compensation as restitution for his past crimes.

But all is not lost for Mr. Leeson. He has benefited from people's morbid fascination with ex–white-collar criminals. After having his exploits immortalized in the film *Rogue Trader*, Leeson has even become a bit of a cult icon among the British. Which movie star played the ignoble Rogue Trader? The same actor who played the noble Obi-Wan Kenobi in the *Star Wars* prequels: Ewan McGregor.

Was Nick Leeson a Right Risk taker? Not even close. In fact, he is Right Risk's antithetical opposite: a Wrong Risk-taker. The risks Leeson took weren't based on any overriding purpose and they weren't grounded on any noble principles. Rather, the risks Leeson took were based on greed and fear. He risked other people's money because he didn't want to lose the lavish lifestyle to which he had grown accustomed.

To *turn on your risk pressure* means to create purposeful anxiety so as to help nudge yourself off your risk platform. The pressure points just discussed can be used to pressure you into taking the risks that will help close the gap between where you are and where you want to be. But beware. Use only as much pressure as you need to take your risk, lest, like Nick Leeson, you buckle under the pressure!

Putting Principle 4 Into Practice

🖎 When thinking about past risks, what types of pressure have been particularly effective at getting you to take the risk? What types of pressure have been ineffective?

_____

_____

🖎 *Personal Performance Pressure*: Be clear about what you are trying to prove in taking your big risk, and to whom you are trying to prove it. Write down what standards of excellence you expect of yourself as you pursue your big risk.

_____

_____

🖎 *Peer Pressure*: Create a list of friends or relatives who would hold you accountable to taking this risk. Of those listed, reach out to the person who would hold you most accountable.

_____

_____

✎ *Pressure of Potential Outcomes*: What outcomes are you hoping to derive from taking this risk? What do you stand to gain? Lose? How will taking this risk help you grow and develop as a person?

_____

_____

✎ *Organizational Pressure*: Pressure yourself into taking the risk by identifying those measures that will let you know when you've accomplished your risk-taking objectives. Also, give yourself a deadline for getting off your risk platform. Lastly, create a way to appraise yourself relative to your risk-taking efforts.

_____

_____

Part Three

Relish the
Moment

There is a certain magic atop the high-dive ladder. Though incredibly frightening, it is also fantastically exciting. For a brief moment, you are among the treetops. Up here, the world is more expansive. Up here, the wind blows more vigorously. Up here, you are a little closer to the sun.

The high-dive moment is a solitary moment. The moment all your preparation, and all your effort and anguishing, have led you to. It is the moment you've been waiting for, your chance to shine. It is *your* moment. Though it is a moment intense with fear, this is not a moment to be rushed through. It is a moment to be *relished!*

Life is one long procession of risks. But during our lives, only a handful of risks are truly destiny-changing. These are moments that, once passed, make up life's reminiscence. The purpose of this part is to help you relish these giant leap moments, as you are taking them, instead of longing for them once they've gone.

Principle 5, *Put Yourself on the Line,* talks about how our personal investment in the risk goes up to the extent that we have some "skin in the game." By managing the genetically coded impulse to preserve ourselves, we can learn to relish our intense risk moments.

Principle 6, *Make Your Fear Work for You,* explains how fear, properly contained, can be converted into excitement, making your risk more enjoyable.

Principle 7, *Have the Courage to Be Courageous,* describes the nature of courage and how essential it is when taking your big risk.

Put Yourself on the Line

❋

"*The progress of an artist is a continual self-sacrifice, a continual extinction of personality.*

—T. S. Eliot

"*Every act of creation is first of all an act of destruction.*"

—Picasso

Woven into the DNA of every living creature, from the tiniest jellyfish to the largest sequoia, is the impulse to live. No creature desires to extinguish itself. Every organism is equipped with the ability to propagate itself in order to ensure the preservation of its genes. Death is to be avoided, and all the things that extend life are held at a premium. Every species must reproduce and then protect its offspring to ensure survival. The basic instinctual knowledge shared by all of creation is that life is preserved most effectively by avoiding danger. Because it is so essential to the perpetuation of life, self-preservation is the most basic and deeply rooted inhibitor of risk.

Were it not for the vital safety mechanism of self-preservation, the alternative, self-destruction, would be the norm. Thus, in writing about self-preservation as an inhibitor of risk, I don't want to suggest that you purposely ward off self-preservation by becoming self-destructive. Rather, I want you to consider the degree to which self-preservation regulates your behavior. Ideally, you should be regulating this powerful instinct versus letting it regulate you. The simple fact is, if your life is governed solely by a desire to avoid danger, you will never be fully expressed as a risk-taker, and you will never be able to relish the risk. Life's greatest risk moments demand that you be willing to relinquish at least a part of your self-preservation instinct, not in a self-destructive way, but in a self-ignoring, or even self-sacrificing way. Thus the fifth Right Risk principle is to *put yourself on the line*.

Self-Preservation

Stand on the edge of a cliff and tilt forward. What happens? Thankfully, the invisible hand of self-preservation rocks you back in place. Without this unseen protector, you would fall off the edge and die. But sometimes self-preservation holds you back, even in safe places. In these instances you are not graced by a benevolent protector, but enslaved under the strict control of a punitive headmaster. And headmaster is exactly the role that self-preservation often assumes. It can lord over your mind, directing every action toward protecting you from danger, until even the slightest risk is viewed as threatening. In the worst cases, the desire to preserve yourself becomes a straightjacket where every move must be painstakingly planned and predicted, and where caution and carefulness hold greater importance than unfettered enjoyment. This preservationist's fear-based approach to life underpins such things as neurosis, paranoia, hypochondria, and agoraphobia. To them, life is something to be contained, not enjoyed.

It is not that seasoned risk-takers discard self-preservation entirely. They are not suicidal. Rather, they refuse to be controlled by it. They recognize that enjoyment comes at a price, and the price is often the acknowledgment and acceptance of your own mortality. As high divers, for example, we were all well aware that every dive carried a real, albeit remote, chance of injury or death. Except for the 30 stitches I got after falling off the stage in Texas, I never got hurt. But many of my buddies did. I recall, for example, joining our troupe at Six Flags Over Georgia the day after one of our divers broke both of his ankles after performing a 60-foot high dive into an 8-foot pool. Everyone knew that taking these unusual risks was an unnatural act and that injury (or worse) came with the territory. The price of admission to all that temporary excitement was the miniscule chance of certain death. It is not that high divers are not afraid to die, it's just that they are not afraid to live. They would rather risk the possibility of death while embracing life's fullness of spirit than live a dispirited death-avoiding life.

Risking Your Reputation

A Right Risk often requires that you offer up your reputation as collateral against the potential rewards the risk might bring. When you do, the stakes become much higher and much more personal. With your reputation on the line, potential losses now include a piece of yourself. A good example of someone who took such a risk is Susan Estrich. As a young Phi Beta Kappa student at Wellesley, Estrich was known for her brilliance and skills of persuasion, qualities that later enabled her to be selected as the first woman president of the *Harvard Law Review* in 1976. Later, in 1981, these same qualities were instrumental in her being selected as a Harvard Law School professor.

But amidst her growing public renown, she was grappling with a private anguish. During her years as a student, she had been violently raped. This event caused her to take a keen interest in U.S. rape laws, which she viewed as victimizing women by placing an unreasonable emphasis on the conduct of the female victim rather than the male perpetrator. Wanting to be instrumental in bringing about change on the issue, Estrich wrote an exhaustive critical treatment of U.S. rape laws for the prestigious *Yale Law Journal*. However, in what was considered a highly unorthodox move, Estrich put her reputation on the line by disclosing her own hardship. The article begins, "Eleven years ago, a man held an ice pick to my throat and said: 'Push over, shut up, or I'll kill you.' I did what he said, but couldn't stop crying. A hundred years later, I jumped out of the car as he drove away."[1]

By disclosing her rape, Estrich was taking the risk of opening up her life to the scrutiny and judgment of the academic establishment. It was entirely possible that Harvard could have viewed her efforts as too audacious and out of the traditional bounds of academic research that at the time frowned upon mixing doctrinal discourse with personal insight. Further adding to her risk, Estrich had written the article in the same year that she was up for tenure. But for Estrich, staking her reputation in order to influence unfair rape laws was a risk worth taking. Happily, not only was she awarded tenure, but the article won critical acclaim. Moreover, as a result of Estrich's Right Risk, the attention in rape cases is now more balanced, with greater focus on the conduct of the alleged perpetrator.

Perhaps, like Susan Estrich, your risk involves putting your reputation at stake. Such risks are frightful—and certainly hard to relish—because we spend a lot of time trying to "preserve our reputations." But in staking your reputation, you affirm your belief in yourself. You are essentially saying that you have enough confidence to trust your inclinations. In these instances, even if the outcome goes horribly wrong and your reputation is tarnished, you can at least live with the satisfaction that you didn't betray yourself by living in a compromised way.

Identity Destruction

Some of the most challenging risks are those that disrupt other people's views of your identity. For example, converting from one religious denomination to another or switching political parties may be seen as highly offensive to the group you are leaving behind. In these instances, the group is likely to view your conversion as a rejection of an identity that they helped create, thus they take it personally. The more orthodox and close-knit the community you are leaving, the more of an outcast you are likely to become. By putting yourself on the line, you disrupt other people's interpretation of who you should be and subject yourself to tremendous derision. You may be viewed as a maverick, rebel, or worse yet, traitor.

Such was the case, for example, in May 2001, when Vermont Senator Jim Jeffords stunningly announced that after serving 14 years in the House and 13 years in the Senate, he was leaving the Republican Party. Making the announcement even more shocking was that in becoming an Independent, Jeffords was shifting the balance of power from a Senate of 50 Republicans and 50 Democrats (with Vice President Cheney in the tie-breaker position for the GOP) to 49 Republicans and 50 Democrats, and one sympathetic Independent (Jeffords). Immediately the GOP labeled Jeffords a turncoat, with some members even going so far as to call him Benedict Arnold. But for Jeffords, upsetting the GOP was the Right Risk to take because it was an act of conscience. A long-time moderate, Jeffords had grown uncomfortable with the GOP's increasingly conservative stance over issues like the environment, abortion rights, and education.

Said Jeffords, "I knew that the unique circumstances of our time would allow one person to walk across the aisle and dramatically change the power structure of government, to again give moderation and balance to the system."[2]

Regardless of your political persuasion (I myself am a Republocrat), it is hard to deny that Jeffords staked his political career for what he believed to be right. As one Senatorial colleague of Jeffords noted, "He was willing to risk his career, friendships, and relationships in a great act of courage." No matter how you view it, Jeffords clearly put himself on the line.

Like Jeffords, when you take the risk of putting forth a truer version of yourself, there will be plenty of people who will ridicule your new identity. But in discarding an identity that no longer suits you, you get to participate in your own evolution. To stifle this process, particularly to please others, would be to stunt your own maturation by going against the grain of nature.

Learning to Risk, Risking to Learn

Let's face it, sometimes the only reason that you put yourself *on* the line is because someone shoved you *over* the line. Not all risks can be planned and well thought out. Not all risks are afforded the luxury of time. Sometimes we are forced to react quickly, relying on our instincts to see us through. For this reason, maintaining a regular risk regimen will increase your risk fitness so that when risks are thrust upon you, you will be better prepared to handle them intuitively. At the same time, just the act of taking risks prepares you for more risk. In going through an intense risk experience, you stretch your capability—and perhaps even your need—for more risk.

Take, for example, Josh Ryker. At 20 years old, like a lot of people his age, he is an extreme sports enthusiast. He has skydived, jumped off waterway bridges, dodged trees on a snowboard while racing at 45 mph, and even tried "reverse bungee jumping"—a bungee apparatus that yanks people upward instead of downward. As would be expected, Josh wears the war wounds of an extreme risk-taker. He has separated his shoulder, bloodied his nose, sprained both of his ankles, and had so many concussions that he lost count. His live-life-to-the-fullest verve may have been perfectly suited for—and perhaps influenced by—his biggest, and most harrowing risk experience: tackling a murderer.

In 1998, Josh and his brother Jake were students at Thurston High School in Springfield, Oregon. Both were on the football team, both were Boy Scouts, and both were very different from Kip Kinkel, the loner student who had been kicked off the football team some time earlier. On May 21, 1998, Jake and Josh were eating in the school cafeteria when Kinkel came in wearing a trench coat and started shooting at everyone in sight. Jake Ryker was shot in the chest just as he stood up to warn his fellow students. He was shot again in the hand when he moved toward Kinkel. Then Josh, in an effort to stop the bloodshed, tackled and subdued Kinkel, with the help of a few teammates. When it was all over, two students lay dead and 25 more lay wounded. Without Josh's heroics, the death toll would have assuredly been higher. Kinkel had lost his mind; he had shot and killed his parents the day before.

It is hard to tell whether Josh Ryker would be such an extreme risk-taker today had he not been through such a life-threatening (and risk-stretching) experience back in 1998. On the other hand, he may have been among the few people at the school who was temperamentally suited for such an act of bravery. Research suggests that our risk-taking behavior is shaped both by the temperament we are born with and the risk knowledge we acquire along the way. Yes, risk-taking, too, is a function of both nature and nurture.

The risk-taking aspect of our personality is evident even in infants, before any external influence would have had time to take effect. At as little as two weeks old, some toddlers have been found to have a greater need for stimuli, such as being more interested in a baby's rattle, or more apt to follow a red ball with their eyes. The same children also appear more alert and less fearful.[3] These inquisitive toddlers may well grow up into adults who drive in life's fast lane, seeking out excitement. Yet, even for those less genetically predisposed to taking risks, the act of taking small risks seems to lead to wanting to take progressively larger ones. Once we learn to ride a bike, we eventually want to try riding with no hands. As we learn to successfully deal with risky situations, they stop being risky, and we desire even greater risk challenges.

Regardless of whether the Ryker brothers were being influenced by nature or nurture, one thing is certain—each put his life on the line to save others. For their acts of heroism both Josh and Jake Ryker were awarded the Boy Scouts' Honor Medal. Kip Kinkel was sentenced to 112 years without parole.

Self-Sacrifice: Chancing Death to Extend Life

Great deeds are wrought at great risk, and human advancement is very often a function of self-sacrifice. History is replete with examples that show that the best way to preserve life is often by chancing death. Sometimes the sole reason for putting yourself on the line is so others won't have to. Consider, for example, one of the great scientific achievements of our age: the eradication of the polio virus.

In the 1950s, summers were a time of fear for parents across the country because of the dreaded disease of the young called *infantile paralysis*. Mothers would warn their kids to stay away from the local pond, a breeding ground for the deadly virus. Movie theaters would show public service reels with young children wearing leather and metal braces, or hospitalized children hooked up to scary looking contraptions called iron lungs. Ushers would then walk through the theater aisles collecting money for the March of Dimes, which was originally founded to gather research funds to combat the crippling disease. Most people knew of someone who had contracted the virus, and if they didn't know someone personally, they at least knew about the most famous polio victim of all—President Franklin Delano Roosevelt.

In 1952, some 58,000 cases of polio were reported, 3,000 of them fatal. With the virus now reaching epidemic proportions, the race was on to develop a vaccine. Dr. Jonas Salk had spent years researching the virus and had developed a concoction that he thought just might work. His experimental vaccine was made from an inactive version of the virus, but without testing the vaccine on humans, Salk could not know for sure whether or not it would work. Convinced of the vaccine's merit, Salk put himself on the line by injecting himself with the experimental vaccine. Riskier still, he also injected it into his wife . . . and three young sons. Fortunately the vaccine worked.

Dr. Salk's successful trial inspired others to try the vaccine. Then in 1954, the largest experimental vaccination in history was performed as roughly 1.8 million school children signed up to become "polio pioneers." The vaccination was a resounding success. Before long, polio was virtually eradicated in every country where the vaccine was administered. Years later, when famed reporter Edward R. Murrow asked Salk who owned the vaccine's patent, in true Right Risk fashion, Salk replied, "Well, the people, I would say," adding, "There is no patent. Could you patent the sun?"[4]

Dr. Salk's self-sacrifice, while notable, is by no means the only example of resisting the impulse of self-preservation in the service of scientific advancement. During the 18th century, another anti-preservationist, Scottish surgeon John Hunter, infected himself with gonorrhea to understand the disease better. Drawing on his unconventional methods of self-experimentation, Hunter published *Treatise on the Venereal Disease,* an important medical work during its day.[5] (Not all acts of self-sacrifice turn out so well. During later experiments in which he tried to prove that syphilis and gonorrhea are different strains of the same disease, Hunter unintentionally gave himself syphilis with fatal results.[6]) In each of these instances, life was preserved at a macro level through self-sacrifice at a micro one by people who were willing to put themselves at risk.

What Makes a Hero?

It is easiest to relish our giant leap moments when we know that our motives for taking the risk are "all true." The word *right*—as in *Right* Risk—implies correct, of pure motive, and full of integrity. In short, *right* equates with *true*. When our motives are "all true," much of our intrinsic satisfaction stems from knowing that we are operating out of our uncompromised, and therefore "truest," self.

Altruism is the purest form of Right Risk, and no one exemplifies this as much as the hero. It is not just the fact that heroes put themselves on the line, it is their motives for doing so. Interestingly, heroes do not share characteristics commonly assigned to risk-takers. Unlike people who take decidedly Wrong Risks, like substance abusers (who also put themselves on the line), heroes are not especially susceptible to boredom, emotionally arousable, disinhibited, or pleasure-seeking. Unlike, say, rock climbers, heroes are not particularly driven by the physiological thrills associated with cheating death. Rather, heroes are driven by something *other*. One study of police officers and firefighters who had been decorated for bravery showed that heroes actually scored *lower* on one of the most studied dimensions of risk-taking: sensation-seeking. It appears that heroes are merely ordinary people who put themselves in extraordinary situations. Why? For reasons described as "pro social" (for the good of others) and altruistic.[7] Perhaps this is why, following a heroic episode, heroes often humbly explain, "I just did what I thought was *right*."

Putting Principle 5 into Practice

✎ What about yourself are you willing to put on the line in taking your big risk? Your reputation? Credibility? Identity? Life?

_____

_____

✎ What about your identity is likely to change as a result of taking your big risk?

_____

🖎 Draw a risk-taking continuum with self-preservation at one pole, and self-sacrifice at the other. Place a mark at the point on the continuum that best reflects your risk posture.

|——|

Self-preservation   *Self-sacrifice*

🖎 Have you ever experienced a change of identity, such as a religious or a political conversion? If so, what about the experience was risky? Which people most resented your change of identity?

_____

_____

🖎 Think about your risk history. What have you learned about risk along the way? Were you born with your present risk disposition or was it molded by experience?

_____

_____

🖎 Make a list of people you think of as heroes. What risks did they take to gain hero status in your eyes? What characteristics do they have that you'd like to emulate? What, if anything, about your risk is altruistic?

_____

_____

Make Your Fear Work for You

"Fear is a question. What are you afraid of, and why? Just as the seed of health is in illness, because illness contains information, your fears are a treasure house of self-knowledge if you explore them."

—Marilyn Ferguson

"Our doubts are traitors,
And makes us lose the good we oft might win
By fearing to attempt."

—William Shakespeare

The most common question asked of high divers is, "Are you afraid up there?" My response has always been that if you aren't afraid, you'll probably get hurt. High divers aren't fearless. Rather, they are fear-enhanced, or *en*feared. It is precisely this fear that heightens a diver's awareness of his surroundings so he won't make any mistakes. Divers often talk of having a "healthy respect for the ladder." We respected the fact that at any time, the high diving gods could cause us to tumble out of control and come crashing down to Earth. Our respect was grounded in fear, and most diving injuries happened in fear's absence. We knew that fear kept us safe. Indeed, we were more worried when we weren't afraid than when we were. When leaping from the ladder, fear was a VIP passenger that always came along for the ride.

When you talk about risk, invariably you have to talk about fear. Risk, after all, has an intimate relationship with fear. Fear is the great risk inhibitor. We *fear* high places. We *fear* loss. We *fear* failure. We *fear* success. We *fear* rejection. We *fear* embarrassment. We *fear* commitment. We *fear* intimacy. We *fear* the unknown. And, of course, we *fear* fear. But the truth about fear is that we need it. Fear is the primary (and primordial) warning system that alerts us to danger. In threatening situations, fear jacks up our heartbeat and stimulates our senses to keep us from getting hurt. In well-proportioned measures, it can sharpen your focus, quicken your reflexes, enhance your performance, and even add to your excitement and enjoyment of the risk. The point is, fear is a powerful energy that, properly channeled, can make risk-taking an invigorating and rewarding experience. Indeed, fear-laden risks tend to be the most memorable once taken. For these reasons, and because relishing risk is partly a function of living in a fear-respectful way, every Right Risk-taker needs to be well versed in Right Risk principle 6: *make fear work for you.*

Sensational Fear

If you sit with fear long enough, you can become comfortable with it. My friend has Lou Gehrig's disease. She has spent much of the last 20 years confined to a wheelchair, and spends most of her days reading horror novels. I once asked her why she is so fascinated with spooky stories. Her answer was insightful, "Because it makes me *feel alive inside.*" My friend's answer captures why some of us actually like being afraid. As mentioned briefly at the end of Principle 5, many risk-takers demonstrate "sensation-seeking behavior." As the term suggests, these people seek out situations that stimulate their senses and enlarge their ability to feel. More than nearly any other emotion, fear magnifies and sharpens our senses. Fear's ability to make us "feel alive inside" can be powerfully enticing. This allure of fear can draw the sensation-seeker into dangerous situations. After all, it is the fear of getting caught that makes the dangerous liaison so exciting, the fear of getting hurt that makes the dangerous stunt so thrilling, and the fear of wiping out that makes the dangerous dive so exhilarating.

Complacency: The Absence of Fear

Ironically, you are most likely to get hurt in situations that are devoid of fear, because the absence of fear can cause complacency. The U.S. Air Force Demonstration Squadron, the Thunderbirds, are among the military's most elite pilots. Their aerial maneuvers combine a mixture of formation and solo flying, all done at the helm of an F-16 while traveling at lightning speed. Pilots like this aren't the fearful type. Mostly that's a good thing. They wouldn't be able to perform with confidence and precision if they were under the grip of fear. But the Air Force knows that at least some level of fear is healthy. For this reason, officer assignments with this elite squadron are limited to two years.[1] Beyond that, the positive effects of fear can wear off altogether, significantly increasing the possibility of a midair catastrophe.

The antecedent of complacency is often success. A

disturbing example of this has recently been noticed in San Francisco where the number of HIV infections has doubled in the last five years. Researchers are so alarmed that the Center for Disease Control recommended—for the first time—that all gay men get screened for HIV at least once a year. The sharp rise in infection was attributed to behavioral complacency brought on by advances in HIV treatment and prevention. Aggressive prevention programs, safe-sex advertising, and better drug treatments were so effective that they had created a "reverse epidemic," whereby the gay community was now lowering its guard against HIV. According to Michael Siever, director of the Stonewall Project, an advocacy group for gay men, "There's much less fear . . . People aren't as careful. They're tired of getting tested and they're tired of the same old campaigns to scare them about sex."[2] In this instance, the consequence of the absence of fear may not just be behavioral complacency, it may be death itself.

Offsetting Complacency with Fear

Even in corporate settings, the total absence of fear can be a sign of danger. In organizations too, complacency can be an outgrowth of success. Bloat follows growth and slows the organization's response to competitive threats. After sustained periods of success, organizations are easily lulled into a false sense of security. During these times, an organization is most vulnerable to injury. For example, one reason the Big 3 automakers had such a tough time in the 1970s was because of their success in selling gas-guzzling cars to a market of "conspicuous consumers." Sustained success caused the Big 3 to believe "It has always been this way, therefore it will always be this way."

To prevent organizational complacency, it is precisely at the moments of a company's greatest triumph that senior executives should make fear work for them by stirring the butterflies in the belly of the workforce. Not as fear-mongers, but as fear leaders. Leaders should have a compensatory relationship to followers. When followers are afraid, leaders should calm them down. Conversely, when followers are apathetic, leaders should counterbalance with fear. One of the most dramatic presentations I ever witnessed was given by a senior executive from a large communications company. Using stark and sobering terms, he warned of the competitive threats looming on the company's horizon, even though the company was coming off its most successful year. This exec knew that success today could cause a train wreck tomorrow. Thus, he deliberately *en*feared the workforce to offset the negative effects of complacency.

The Dark Side of Fear

While fear does have some redeeming qualities (like preventing complacency), it would be foolish to suggest that fear is always a performance-enhancing elixir. At a certain point fear converts from a risk-motivating force to a risk-inhibiting rogue. Fear can bludgeon the fledgling risk-taker's courage. I've seen rookie high divers so paralyzed with fear that they were unable to climb to the top and unable to walk back down, literally stuck on the middle of the ladder. When fear tucks under your skin and worms its way into your brain, it assaults your nervous system with adrenaline-filled hand grenades. Left unchallenged, your vital signs become deranged, your heartbeat races, your skin blotches, your vision constricts, you lose your appetite, you sweat profusely, and you hyperventilate. The physiological response itself can be so frightening that you may become more afraid of your fearful feelings than you are of the risk that prompted them. You are in a panic attack, the fear of fear itself.

A friend of mine is a Vietnam veteran. He recently confided to me that he sometimes misses combat. He explained that the fury of combat had taught him things about his character that he hadn't known existed, things like valor, honor, and courage. Further, it taught him that fear, like electricity, can provide the needed energy to help you take a risk. For many of the same reasons previously mentioned—focus, alertness, excitement—he and his fellow soldiers believed it was good to be scared. But before each major offensive they would tell each other, "Don't let the fear getcha." As he explained, if the fear "gotcha," it resulted in a macabre paralysis that would electrocute you in its grip. Under the spell of fear, a soldier would be frozen on his gun's trigger, unable to squeeze and unable to release, just a sitting target.

At issue is how to achieve the right balance of fear, so that you can make it work for you. Not enough fear, and the risk is banal and boring (and—one could argue—not really a risk). Too much fear, and the risk is nearly impossible to take. You are most apt to take a risk when the dose of fear is strong enough to motivate you into action, but not so strong that it stuns your nerves. Beyond a certain point, fear can have diminishing returns.

Fear of the Unknown

A lot has been written about the natural tendency to fear the unknown. In my opinion, the first (and perhaps best) description of this phenomenon comes from the 4000-year-old masterpiece of Plato. In *The Republic*, Socrates (an early Right Risk-taker) describes fear as being a function of knowledge versus ignorance. He draws an interesting parallel between the nature of dogs and humans, explaining that a dog will bark at a stranger regardless of whether the stranger has ever harmed him, but will be gentle with someone he knows, whether or not he has received kindness from him. Socrates notes that "knowing and not knowing are the sole criteria the dog uses to distinguish friend from enemy."[3]

Humans, too, will bark at what is foreign. What we are ignorant of, we are often afraid of. Consequently, the most unfamiliar things are often first viewed as a threat, and we put up our defenses. One way to reduce fear (i.e., ignorance) is to increase your exposure to the feared object or situation so that you gain knowledge of it. Psychologists call this the "mere-exposure effect," meaning that we can grow more comfortable with something just by spending time with it. When we acquaint ourselves with our fears, their debilitating effect on us dissipates.

For example, I have a relative who is prejudiced. He

grew up in New York where communities are tightly segmented by ethnic sections (Little Italy, Spanish Harlem, Chinatown, etc.). A few years ago he came to visit me in Atlanta. At the end of his visit, I took him to see the tomb of Martin Luther King, Jr., perhaps Atlanta's most famous hero. We also toured the house where King was raised as a child. What started out as a whim turned out to be a profoundly moving experience for my relative. Having grown up during the tumultuous era of the civil rights movement and having witnessed race riots and looting in New York, he thought of King as a troublemaker and inciter. But standing in King's home, seeing where he ate, bathed, and slept made King more relatable. King the man was more accessible than King the provocative political figure. A simple tour of King's home did more to reduce my relative's prejudiced views than any finger-pointing on my part could have done. Seeing the ordinary man behind the extraordinary hero helped convert my relative's ignorance into knowledge.

As Socrates suggested, and as my relative experienced, fear changes from an enemy to a friend to the extent that you move from a condition of *not knowing* to *knowing*. And it is hard to know things you keep at a distance. Instead, relishing your risk requires that you spend time "merely-exposed" to your risk. Thinking about starting a business? Take a weekend apprenticeship in the same field. Thinking about moving overseas? Take an extended trip abroad. You will remain hampered by fear of the unknown only as long as you remain loyal to your ignorance.

Fear of the Known

In my opinion, fear of the unknown is overrated. The real fear, and the hardest to overcome, is fear of the *known*. Few things inhibit our ability to take a risk as much as an early bad experience. In these instances, you know all too well the consequences of a risk . . . and you've got the scars to prove it. For example, I am an avid whitewater kayaker. A few years ago, while paddling Tennessee's famed Ocoee River, I got flipped upside down in a rapid affectionately known as

"Grumpy." Kayakers label rapids based on reputation, a linguistic expression of homage to man's collective risk experience. Some names are friendly, like "Surprise" or "Cat's Pajamas," other names are more ominous, like "Decapitation Rock," "Table Saw," or "Witch's Hole." Grumpy got its name for a reason—this nasty hydraulic is as friendly as a grizzly bear with hemorrhoids. By obsessing solely about Grumpy's dangerous consequences, I lost my composure and exited my kayak. In fast moving whitewater, the safest place to be is in your boat, even if you're upside down. It is when you are orphaned from your boat that you are most exposed to rocks. As I bobbled up and down the fast river, I felt as if I was in a liquid pinball game, banging into rocks with every body part. By the time Grumpy was through trashing me, I was bruised all over.

After my little brawl with Grumpy, whenever my buddies and I would go paddling, I would shamefully trudge my boat past Grumpy and enter the water farther downstream. Before long, years had gone by since the episode, but I was still trudging my boat past the rapid. I was in full fear of the known. Whereas the antidote to fear of the unknown is gaining knowledge, the antidote to fear of the known is a mixture of willful ignorance and focused attention. The truth was, unless I could stop mentally replaying the beating I had taken years earlier, I would never get past my fear of Grumpy. At the same time, I would have to pinpoint exactly what had gone wrong so that I could do it differently.

When I finally did paddle through Grumpy again, instead of thinking about all the things that could go wrong, I focused on the specific actions that I needed to take to successfully navigate the rapid. When you look at Grumpy in its entirety, it is incredibly intimidating. Water crashes onto boulders, rushes through narrow confluences, and circulates beneath undercut rocks. But successfully navigating Grumpy comes down to an intermediate ferry move. Ferrying is when you use the river's current to move from one side of the river to the other while facing upstream. By focusing with laser-like attention on making the ferry move, and not on Grumpy's tumultuous panorama, I was able to conquer the rapid and my fear too.

Caging Fear

There is little physiological distinction between intense feelings of fear and excitement; they are neurological correlates. What happens when you are afraid? Your heart quickens, your blood pressure builds, your stomach teems with butterflies, your breathing shortens, and your skin tingles with nervous energy, right? Now, what happens when you are about to have sex? Enough said.

Though physiologically fear and excitement are nearly indistinguishable, there is one simple but profound difference. We experience fear as unpleasant, and excitement as pleasant. Fear can lead to feelings of anxiety, dread, apprehension, and terror. These feelings might be prompted by sitting in a dentist's chair or being summoned by the IRS. Conversely, excitement is accompanied by feelings of joy, euphoria, and even ecstasy. These feelings might be aroused by winning a thrilling athletic victory or getting an acceptance letter from the college of your choice. The more intense the fear the more unpleasant it feels, and the more intense the excitement the more pleasant it feels. The real question becomes, *what if you could use all the raw physiological energy aroused when you're afraid, and convert it into excitement?* You can. In fact you already do.

The truth is we enjoy, and even seek out, a good fright. Of our own free will we will do scary things, not in spite of the associated fear, but because of it. We will skydive, hang glide, ride motor cross, and go shark fishing for no other reason than scary enjoyment. Out of all God's creatures, man is the only one known to seek out danger just for fun's sake.

The most thrilling situations are those that fuse the emotions of fear and excitement closely together. Indeed, the most basic objective of an amusement park is to make you *scream* with *joy*. Notice that your enjoyment isn't contingent upon a reduction in fear's intensity. To the contrary, the more fear-saturated the better. The most inviting roller coaster is the colossal beast at the far edge of the park, the giant loop-d-loop monster that promises to thrash you to and fro at G-force speed. We are no longer satisfied with sitting passively on a soft cushiony seat. We want to ride the beast standing straight up. Better yet, take the floor away and let our feet dangle over the asphalt below!

Rather than fight fear, make it work for you by using all that combustible energy to embolden your spirit and fuel your ability to take, and enjoy, the risk. You do this not by reducing the fear's intensity, but by increasing the robustness of what British psychologist Dr. Michael Apter calls your "protective frame." In his fascinating book, *The Dangerous Edge*, Apter provides a useful metaphor for understanding this concept. He writes, "Think of looking at a tiger in a cage. Both the tiger *and* the cage are needed in order to experience excitement: The tiger without the cage would be frightening; the cage without the tiger would be boring. Both are necessary. In order to experience excitement, then, we need both the possibility of danger and something we believe will protect us from it."[4]

As Apter explains, many situations can potentially arouse feelings of excitement or anxiety depending on how safe you believe yourself to be. The safer we feel, the more we can cope with fearful feelings. In other words, fear does not *always* have to have diminishing returns. As long as the danger of our risk is matched in equal measure by something that increases our safety, our fear will be offset with excitement. Thus, Apter suggests that instead of reducing the size of the tiger (fear), you should strengthen the metal of the cage (protective frame). Fear is converted to excitement to the degree that you build up your confidence and capability. When you seek out coaching, are well rehearsed, deepen your skills, have strong social support, and have safe equipment, you become emboldened by feelings of confidence, greatly enhancing your chances of withstanding fear's debilitating effects. The more robust the protective frame, the more ferocious the tiger you can deal with, and the more scary fun you can have!

Pulling Back the Curtain

When we are faced with fear, our first instinct is often to run away. We are not unlike the cowardly lion in *The Wizard of*

Oz, who, when looking at the menacing image of the great and powerful Oz, hightailed it in the other direction. The impulse to run is reversed, however, when we pull back the curtain on our fears and bring it down to size. Contrary to the Wizard's famous directive, we should indeed pay attention to the man behind the curtain. More often than not, he is smaller than we think.

Putting Principle 6 Into Practice

Think about your past risks. What fears reoccur most consistently?

_____

_____

Think about the risk you are currently faced with. What are you most afraid of?

_____

_____

What is driving your fear, the *known* or the *unknown*? Have you ever had a direct experience with what you are fearing? Or is it an entirely foreign experience?

_____

_____

Take out a piece of paper and draw a line down the middle. On the left-hand side, list all the ways that your fear is actually serving you (e.g., keeping you safe). On the right-hand side, list the ways that the fear is holding you back.

_____

What about your risk secretly excites you? How is your excitement tied to your fear?

_____

_____

 Think about the metaphor of a "tiger in a cage." What is your tiger? How big and ferocious is it? How strong is your cage (protective frame)? What can you do to strengthen it (e.g., get a coach, rehearse, get social support, build your skills)?

_____

_____

Have the Courage to Be Courageous

"Courage is doing what you're afraid to do. There can be no courage unless you're scared."

—Eddie Rickenbacker

". . . God will not have his work made manifest by cowards."

—Ralph Waldo Emerson

The subject of our last principle (fear) and the subject of this principle (courage) go hand-in-hand. Fear is the predecessor, and instigator, of courage. Indeed, because courage is a response to fear, you can't demonstrate courage unless you are afraid. Though people falsely assume that courage is about being fearless, in reality the opposite is true. Courage is completely *full* of knee-knocking, teeth-chattering fear. So rather than walk with the cocksure swagger of John Wayne, courage shakes with the insecure awkwardness of Barney Fife.

The difference between a coward and a courageous person is not that one is afraid and the other isn't. To be sure, both are afraid. Rather, the difference is in how each *responds* to fear. To be a coward is to turn and run from fear when you are fully capable of confronting it, but unwilling to do so. Conversely, to be courageous is to stay and confront fear even though you are afraid, not with Neanderthal bravery, mind you, but by allowing yourself to stay present with all your fearful feelings and then to walk through them. Even though courage is full of fear, *it takes the risk anyway.* By definition then, courage means acting in the face of fear.

When we demonstrate courage, the best of ourselves emerges, and our character is displayed. Self-satisfaction comes from knowing that we are doing something that is difficult for us. Relishing our risk moment comes naturally when we follow Right Risk principle 7: *Have the courage to be courageous.*

Courage and Cowardice

Fear is like a schoolyard bully who stands in front of you, shoves your shoulder and says, *So what are you going to do about it?* In essence, the question is a provocation—a dare—

that confronts you with a choice between demonstrating courage or succumbing to cowardice. For this reason, in situations where fear is the only thing standing in the way of getting something you want, dealing with fear should be viewed as an opportunity to strengthen your courage.

For example, I once coached a professional named Bob who was considering three separate job offers. All were well-known companies, but one was of particular renown. Its name carried a certain pedigree that eclipsed the others. Bob had settled his mind on one of the lesser offers, rationalizing that this particular job most resembled the roles that he had had in the past—roles that no longer challenged him, as he had mentioned in the course of earlier discussions. Sensing there was more to it, I asked him to describe his impressions about the more prominent company. He said that many of the people who worked there had Ivy League degrees (which he didn't) and/or graduate degrees (which he had). Although they had offered him the job, he said that he was *afraid* he wouldn't cut it. I now understood that the issue wasn't about skill compatibility; it was about Bob's personal insecurities, it was about his fear. I probed further, "Bob, what *exactly* are you afraid of?" He thought for a second and said, "I guess I am afraid that everyone will be smarter than me, that my ideas won't be valued. If that happens, they'll fire me." Directed by Bob's answer, I asked him another, more courage-provoking, question: *If fear weren't an issue, which job would you choose?* Without hesitation he selected the one he was most afraid of.

As Bob's story illustrates, fear often indicates something about yourself that you are avoiding. Left unaddressed, life will bombard you with a litany of opportunities to confront these "issues" until you finally resolve them. Each time you avoid the issue, you stuff it further into your psyche. But knowing that dealing with the issue represents your growth, your psyche throws the issue back up until you finally confront it, as if to say, *if you don't learn the lesson, you have to repeat the class*. Through coaching, Bob was able to see that not only did the job he was afraid of represent an opportunity to gain experience working in a world-class organization, but it also represented an ideal opportunity to explore and, more importantly, to overcome his deep-rooted feelings of low self-worth. But to benefit from both opportunities, he would have to muster up the courage to be courageous and to face his fear. Ultimately he did. He chose the opportunity he was most afraid of.

Courage Capability

Any risk situation has a grand continuum: You are either moving in the direction of your courage or moving in the direction of your cowardice. When you face your fears, your *Courage Capability* expands, enlarging your capacity for dealing with future fears. In this way, demonstrating courage is itself a form of *en*couragement in that it fills you with greater levels of courage. Fortified with more courage, you are then capable of facing more fearful situations. For example, as a young professional you might find it petrifying to give a presentation to ten people. However, as you progress in your career and gain more experience with public speaking, you are able to comfortably address larger and larger audiences. In this example, the number of additional audience members reflects the degree of expansion of your *Courage Capability*.

Of course the opposite is also true. In situations where you allow fear to prevent yourself from having something you want, you enlarge your *Cowardice Capability*. And the more cowardice you exhibit, the more it grows because cowardice feeds on the diminishment of courage. On a certain level, this is also quantifiable. For example, the person who is afraid to take the risk of asking for a raise can calculate his cowardice as the difference between his current salary and the adjusted salary he feels he deserves but is too afraid to ask for (assuming, of course, that he would have gotten the raise).

People don't like using the word *coward*. They look for softer, less offensive terms. But just because we don't like the word doesn't mean cowardice isn't real. Cowardice is as real as courage. One exists in relation to the other. Furthermore, just as there have been times in your life when you've been courageous, the chances are, at some point in your life you've been a coward as well. Most acts of cowardice, however, go unnoticed and remain concealed within the confines of your heart. Cowardice comes in compromising your principles, in allowing your boundaries to be crossed, in failing to demonstrate personal fidelity, and in not taking a stand for what you believe in. You could spend your whole life being a coward and no one would know it but you.

Having the courage to be courageous means backing up courageous actions with a courageous attitude. It means holding a clear picture of yourself being courageous and continuously asking yourself, *how would the courageous person I want to become act in this fearful situation that I am faced with today?* It means first believing in the virtue of courage and then acting in a courageous manner. When it comes to courage, you have to *believe* it to *be* it.

The Courage to Confront Yourself

Demonstrating courage often means accepting your limitations. For example, once while performing in a high-diving show at Adventureland in Des Moines, Iowa, I was forced to accept my limitations in front of 2,000 people. With a moderate wind, all high-dive ladders will sway. But as I climbed to the top of the ladder, I noticed that it was swaying with more vigor than usual. It was a balmy August day and winds were gusting out of the Northwest. Just as I let go of the ladder and readied for the dive, a strong burst of wind sideswiped me from the right, shoving me sideways to the left and almost off the platform. *Oh my God!* I thought as my right hand instinctively reached for the ladder behind me. Had my hand missed, I would have plummeted to the concrete deck ten stories below. Startled, all those gut-curdling fear responses became activated inside me. It took every ounce of composure I had not to have a full-blown panic attack.

Experience had taught me that in moments of panic, the best way to regain composure is to pay attention to my breathing. There is something comforting in the measured rhythms of inhaling and exhaling. However, the combination of the spastic winds, the sway of the ladder, and the urging eyes of the audience were particularly taxing on me. Though at this point in my diving career I had about a thousand high dives under my belt, this was like nothing I'd ever experienced. I was way out of my comfort zone. I was perplexed. *Should I try to do the dive between gusts?* I thought. If I could time it right, it would be unlikely that the wind would push me off my trajectory once I got in the air. *Should I climb back down?* It would be pretty embarrassing to have to slither down the ladder in front of a full house of park patrons. Beyond that, I'd have to endure the endless ribbing of my teammates. At the same time, there was something queer about this moment. It just didn't feel *right*.

Of all the things that the discipline of diving gave me, the one thing I am most grateful for is "the voice." Diving taught me to trust the little voice inside me that, like the Little Engine That Could, says, "I think I can." I believe it's the voice of courage. The high-dive platform can be a lonely place, and often the little courageous voice—my inner advocate—was my most loyal companion. I asked myself, *What's the* right *thing to do?* My little internal voice whispered back, *What do you want?* I answered, *I want to be safely on the ground.* It was clear, more than anything else I wanted to be *safe.* And the safe thing to do was obvious. With that, I saluted the audience, gingerly turned around, and started descending back down the ladder. In 7 years performing in front of audiences as large as 50,000 people, no crowd ever roared with approval as much as they did that day. As one relieved audience member told me later, "We were as nervous as you were!"

The Courage to Say No

Risk for risk's sake is arrogance, not courage. Often the most courageous acts are acts of risk restraint. Restraint doesn't mean resignation or cowardice. Exercising restraint is not running away from fear. Rather, it means putting your risk motor in neutral and waiting for a better alignment between the risk opportunity and your capabilities. It reflects a poised composure that is capable of idling the lower appetites of hubris and greed. To act with occasional risk restraint is to exhibit risk maturity. Above all, acting with restraint involves accepting and embracing the reality of your limitations. You can only relish your risk moment if you are alive to relish it, and passing on a risk today may better prepare you to engage in a risk tomorrow. Some of your most dignified and edifying risk moments are when you bow gracefully to the risk gods and say, *"Today is your day . . . but I will be back tomorrow."*

In every field or endeavor, the most exceptional risk-takers are those who can resist the lower urges of the moment in order to satisfy the higher aspirations of the future. Few people exemplify this as much as Ed Viesturs. In December 2000, *Outside Magazine* selected 25 of the best adventure All-Stars. Ed topped the list. According to the article, Ed has summitted eleven of the world's fourteen 8,000-meter peaks. Moreover, he has made nine attempts at Everest—all without oxygen bottles. His legend has grown in part due to the role he played in the ill-fated 1996 Everest climb, which claimed the lives of 8 people and was immortalized in the IMAX film *Everest.* In the course of his own successful climb, Viesturs courageously helped rescue climbers who had become stranded near the summit.

Viesturs's risk maturity is evidenced by his account of his first Everest expedition in 1987, a three-month attempt to climb Everest's famed North Face. As related to *Outside Magazine*, Viesturs said, "So here we are, 300 feet from the summit—spitting distance—and we turned around and walked away. It was a very difficult decision. You've spent years training, months of preparation, thousands of dollars, and you throw it all away. A lot of people are willing to risk their lives. I'm not. We probably could have made it to the top, but with conditions and our abilities, we weren't sure we could make it down. And that's the critical factor. Getting up is optional, getting down is mandatory."[1] He turned away from the summit the following year too. He finally made the summit in 1990 and has now stood on top of the world's highest peak five times. Shakespeare was right: Discretion *is* the better part of valor.

Risk restraint is not always about saying "no" to a risk, it can also be about saying "yes" to safety. This is not always an easy choice because saying yes to safety can tarnish your reputation as a risk-taker. No one likes to look wimpy. On the NASCAR circuit, for example, reputations are made through a mixture of skill and swagger. Few racers embodied this as much as NASCAR legend Dale Earnhardt. No one can deny that he was a skilled racer. In the course of his career he won the season-long Winston Cup title seven times. His skill was made all the more potent by the mystique surrounding his reputation as *the Intimidator*. Earnhardt was a full-throttle risk-taker who wasn't afraid of mouthing off to the risk gods. "Candy asses" was his label for those racers who supported the push to slow down race cars (which adds to the spectator excitement by bunching up the field). Chiding them, he added, "Get the hell out of the race car if you've got feathers on your legs or butt."[2]

But when Earnhardt crashed into the fourth wall at Daytona, his reluctance to say "yes" to safety may have gotten the best of him. He had refused to wear the new Head and Neck Support (HANS) system, a device that curbs whiplash. As of the writing of this book, no NASCAR driver wearing the HANS system has ever died in a crash. Not one.[3] While we will never know if Earnhardt would have survived the crash had he worn the device (his death may have been attributable to a failed seat belt), this much is clear: Had he agreed to wear a safety device—an act of risk restraint—he would have significantly increased his chances of surviving a crash. Earnhardt's fans can take solace in knowing that by losing a racing legend, they gained a risk god.

The Courage to Tell the Truth

Having the courage to be courageous is rarely an easy thing to do; otherwise, there would be more people doing it. Indeed, sometimes the courageous choice, while noble, can exact a toll on your life. Whistleblowers, for example, are among the most courageous Right Risk-takers of all. Why? Because they do something that many other people won't: They tell the truth. But as truth-tellers, they threaten those who would prefer to keep the truth hidden and often become subject to their scorn. By some estimates, as many as half of all whistleblowers lose their jobs, half of those fired will lose their homes, and many will eventually lose their marriages as well.[4] Even those who don't fare as badly can expect some form of reprisal, be it harassment, public humiliation, or even violence. Moreover, because being a whistleblower often carries the stigma of being a snitch or tattletale, even friends and family members may become unsupportive, forcing the whistleblower to go it alone.

In 2002, three huge media stories revolved around the courageous whistleblowing actions of three Right Risk women. First, Sherron Watkins, an accountant with Enron, sent a memo to her boss's boss's boss, warning, "I am incredibly nervous that we will implode in a wave of accounting scandals . . . the business world will consider the past successes as nothing but an elaborate accounting hoax."[5] Then, Coleen Rowley, a legal counsel in the FBI's Minneapolis office, sent a scathing 13-page letter to FBI Director Robert Muller (with copies to the Senate Intelligence Committee), expressing disgust at the way intelligence was handled prior to 9/11, intelligence that she believed might have prevented the tragedy. She observed, "I have deep concerns that a delicate and subtle shading/skewing of the facts by you and others at the highest levels of FBI management has occurred and is occurring."[6] Finally, Cynthia Cooper, an internal auditor at WorldCom, confronted then company CFO Scott Sullivan with evidence of improper accounting practices, practices that when brought to light turned out to be the largest financial fraud in history.[7] In each case, these women put themselves at considerable risk in order to do what they felt was right. For their heroism, the three women were named *Time Magazine's* 2002 Persons of the Year.

Lest you discount the courageousness of these women, consider all the people who might have prevented the tragedies of Enron and WorldCom from happening, had they come forward. There was total silence from the board of directors, the auditing departments, independent accounting firms, and corporate lawyers. In companies as large as these, it would seem highly unlikely that knowledge of these deceptive practices was limited to only one or two key people. More likely, others *did* know but were either afraid of the consequences of disclosure or had too much of a vested interest in seeing the activities continue. Commenting on the surprising lack of truth-telling, that old iconoclastic whistle-blower himself Ralph Nader said, "Would a despot-dictatorship have been more efficient in silencing them and producing the perverse incentives for all to keep quiet? The system is so efficient that there was total silence. I mean, even the Soviet Union had enough dissidents to fill Gulags."[8]

The Battle for Courage

War is perhaps the most terrifying of all human activities. War is a zero-sum contest where the stark consequence of cowardice is death. For this reason and because war is the ultimate fear-inducer, war has been the birthplace of many people's courage. Take, for example, Joseph Foss, who shot down 26 Japanese planes in the Battle of Guadalcanal, an unsurpassed record during WWII. Such bravery helped him get elected governor of South Dakota. Or how about Jefferson De Blanc, who as a fighter pilot in the Solomon Islands destroyed five enemy aircraft in a matter of minutes before his own plane was sent into a tailspin. After parachuting to the ocean, he swam more than 9 miles to a small Japanese-held island and survived there in secret before being rescued two weeks later.[9]

These are only two examples of the incredible stories of the recipients of the U.S. Congressional Medal of Honor, which is bestowed on those individuals who "risk their lives above and beyond the call of duty." As the highest military decoration, it is presented by the President, more than one of whom has whispered to a proud recipient, "I'd rather have that medal than be President of the United States."

While war is often the instigator of courage on the front lines, so, too, is it on the protest lines. And in extremely rare instances, one person displays courage on both fronts. Charles Liteky is such a person. As an Army Chaplain in Vietnam, Liteky carried 23 men to safety while facing fierce machine-gun fire—a feat made all the more remarkable considering that he was wounded in both the neck and foot. For his courage, Liteky was awarded the Medal of Honor. But in a later act of protest, Liteky left his medal at the base of the Vietnam Memorial, forgoing a $600 a month lifetime tax-free pension. The reason? Ironically, for the same reason he won the Medal of Honor: to save lives. Liteky was protesting the U.S.'s sponsorship of the Army's School of the Americas, the controversial school where U.S. officers trained Latin American military personnel. Some, like Liteky, suspected that the school taught torture tactics and trained soldiers in political assassination techniques. In protesting the violent tactics of the school, Liteky was arrested numerous times and, at 70 years old, spent a year in Lompoc federal prison (including a 70-day stint in solitary confinement).[10]

While Liteky's actions may be off-putting to some, his acts of moral conscience have garnered respect from both demonstrators and Army personnel. Even Paul Buch, himself a Medal of Honor recipient and a past president of the Congressional Medal of Honor Society, says, "When I look at Liteky, I have respect for the courage of his views. It is difficult to be an iconoclast. It is much easier to go along. Men like Liteky are people who should cause us to pause and think, they should not be ostracized and criticized. They are entitled to their views, and perhaps if we listened to them we would be better off."[11]

In commenting on his own courage, Liteky explains, "For me now, the most courageous thing has been to be non-violent, to go out and face violence and have the courage not to be violent."[12]

The National Park Service retrieved Charles Liteky's medal and now displays it at the National Museum of American History in Washington, D.C.

The Fall Hike Effect

It takes courage to live in a courageous way. Doing so means continually allowing yourself to experience fearful situations. But the more you courageously face fear, the less intimidating it becomes. I call this the *Fall Hike Effect*. My wife, Shannon, and I enjoy hiking in the mountains of North Georgia, especially during Georgia's short fall season. On these chilly fall days, I'll often get all bundled up to insulate myself from the frigid air. Early on, all my woolen armor helps me brave the cold. But before long, my physical exertion starts to heat up my internal furnace. After a while I am not cold at all, I am *hot*, and I have to start peeling off the layers. My condition is now fully reversed from when I started! In the same way, when facing your fear, your early perceptions about the fear are likely to be very intimidating. However, as you begin exercising your courage, the Fall Hike Effect is likely to kick in, and your cold feelings of fear will turn into warm feelings of excitement. And when they do, you won't fear your risk, you'll relish it.

Putting Principle 7 Into Practice

🖎 How do you define courage? What traits make someone courageous?

_____

_____

🖎 Relative to your big risk, are you moving toward courage or are you moving toward cowardice?

Cowardice   Courage

🖎 Identify some things you can do to enlarge your *Courage Capability*. How would asserting yourself in small situations help you be bolder in more demanding ones?

_____

_____

How would the courageous person you want to become face the fears you are challenged with today?

_____

_____

 Do you consider yourself a truth-teller? What risk have you taken was an act of truth-telling?

_____

_____

 Think about the bravest thing you've ever done. Was it an act of gallantry or an act of protest? In what ways would you like to be braver?

_____

_____

Part Four

Commit to
the Risk

Every risk is comprised of two major decisions. First is the decision of whether or not to *pursue* the risk. Until we decide to pursue the risk, we are "just looking," like curious window shoppers. Our real investment doesn't start until we decide to pursue the risk in earnest. If we follow through on our decision to pursue, eventually we reach a second, more substantial decision, the decision of whether or not to actually *take* the risk. This decision, our *jump* or *don't jump* decision, represents our last chance to back out.

Each decision requires a commitment of us. The *pursue* decision requires an investment of our attention, effort, time, money, etc. The *jump* decision, requires a commitment to follow through with the risk, even if things get tough. Like a bridegroom at the altar, unless you can affirm your decision with a heartfelt "I do," you had better pass on the risk.

For risk-taking to work, a lukewarm commitment won't do. As high divers, for example, once we left the platform, we had to stiffen our bodies so that we wouldn't crumple under the water's striking impact. In the same way, your Right Risk will require a steadfast commitment to withstand the resistance you are likely to encounter. This part looks at some of the commitments that you'll need to make to as you pursue, and take, your risk.

With Principle 8, *Be Perfectly Imperfect,* you'll learn to overcome the risk-inhibiting tendency to want to take mistake-free risks. Principle 9, *Trespass Continuously,* shows you how our commitment to the risk often requires a willingness to be disobedient. Finally, in Principle 10, *Expose Yourself,* you'll read about ways to demonstrate a continued commitment to risk-taking by carrying the Right Risk principles to the more personal areas of your life, by risking self-disclosure.

Be Perfectly Imperfect

"Perfection itself is imperfection."

—Vladimir Horowitz

"Nothing is perfect. There are lumps in it."

—James Kenneth Stephens

"Things out of perfection sail
And all their swelling canvas wear . . ."

—William Butler Yeats

Nobody's perfect, but that doesn't seem to stop people from trying. And why not? There are lots of good reasons for wanting to be perfect. Some professions, for example, greatly benefit from their inherent perfectionism. This is especially true of professions where the consequences of mistakes would be catastrophic, where the human or the financial costs of errors are simply too great to bear. Indeed, the higher the potential for catastrophe, the more necessary and warranted is the perfectionistic behavior. Consequently, among the most perfectionistic people you'll ever meet are bridge-building engineers, skyscraper architects, nuclear physicists, software engineers, and brain surgeons. I, for one, thank God for that. If you ever had the misfortune of requiring brain surgery and had to choose between a pursed-lipped, anal-retentive surgical tactician or a giddy, free-wheeling improvisationalist, who would *you* choose?

The trouble with perfectionism is that it impedes our ability to take risks. Perfectionists are better suited for mitigating risks than for taking them. This mostly stems from their almost obsessive preoccupation with anticipating what can go wrong. Perfectionists are prone to "catastrophizing," focusing on worst-case scenarios in order to account for, and control, every possible negative outcome. This, in turn, lends itself toward a doom-n-gloom outlook when facing a risk. Thus, risks themselves are seen through a prism of negativity that not only makes the risk-taking experience unenjoyable, but through the power of expectancy often sets it up for failure as well. Which brings us to Right Risk Principle 8: *Be perfectly imperfect.* Here you will look at some of the ways that perfectionism interferes with risk-taking, and why making a commitment to being perfectly imperfect is one of the best things you can do while pursuing, and taking, your risk.

The Value of Mistakes

Whether you have decided to pursue your risk, or if you have just jumped off your risk platform, you will have a more difficult time of it if you are a perfectionist. Risk-taking is inherently a mistake-driven process, characterized by a whole lot of trial and a whole lot of error. What perfectionists hate most are mistakes. To perfectionists, a mistake is more than an error; it is a failure that reflects on them personally. You can even hear it in their language. After making a mistake an average person will say something like "My idea didn't work so I tried something else," but a perfectionist will scornfully lament, "I tried my idea and it was an utter failure. I should have known it was a dumb idea. I won't make that mistake again!"

When mistakes equate with failure, risk-taking is viewed as the surest path to dejection and humiliation. Thus the dispositions of perfectionists and risk-takers are often diametrically opposite. These differences are well captured by Dr. Monica Ramirez Basco in her insightful book on perfectionism, *Never Good Enough*. She explains that risk-takers are unlike perfectionists in that they "do not expect themselves to always be right or always have great ideas. But they know that if they keep trying, they will hit upon a winner. If their ideas are rejected, they might get their feelings hurt but they will recover quickly. The consequences of failure for these people do not feel as great as they would to the perfectionist."[1]

Risk-takers view mistakes as an inevitable part of the risk-taking experience. Unlike perfectionists, who categorically assume that perfection is both necessary and attainable, the risk-taker knows better. It is not that risk-takers want to make mistakes. Rather they see mistakes as valuable sources of data that will ultimately help them attain their goals. When someone pointed out to Thomas Edison that in inventing the incandescent light bulb he had performed 10,000 failed experiments, he is purported to have replied, "I have not failed. I just found 10,000 ways that didn't work."

Risk-takers hold the view that, though painful, mistakes are to be expected. In springboard diving, for example, a diver knows that to progress in the sport he or she must take on dives with greater difficulty, literally translated in the sport through a mathematical calculation that signifies each dive's *degree of difficulty,* or what divers refer to as DD. The dives with the highest DD are those with the highest risk. Divers know that in exchange for a repertoire of dives with a higher average DD, they will likely have to endure a bunch of belly flops; welts come with the territory. But they also know that dives with a high DD are those with the biggest potential payoff. At some point in his or her career, a diver will either commit to pursing high DD, or not. And at the elite levels, there are no low DD divers. Likewise, if you want to be a Right Risk-taker, eventually you will have to fully commit yourself to the risk, and all the hardships and imperfections that come with it.

Perfectionism and Control

Perfectionism has few rivals in its ability to push people away. At best, the perfectionist will try to meticulously account for every possible negative outcome, causing them to be painstakingly slow. At worst, they are overdominating and picayune. As the vice president of program services for Executive Adventure, an Atlanta-based experiential team building company, I witnessed many examples of perfectionism's corrosive effects. One example in particular stands out. I was facilitating a strategic planning effort for an international service organization. During the session, one board member, a British chap named Percy, was hindering the group's progress in re-evaluating their strategic direction. Percy was the only executive I ever saw who actually wore an ascot—which complemented his monogrammed blue blazer. Whenever a board member tossed out an idea, Percy would give a look of disdain and condescendingly explain, ad nauseam, why the idea would put the organization at risk. It became apparent that without some type of intervention, the board would leave the planning session having made no progress at all. Rather than confronting Percy directly, I decided to do an experiential activity so that the negative consequences of his perfectionist behavior would be brought to light in a less threatening but more impactful way.

Under the guise of wanting to break up the monotony of the working session, I took them outside to do an activity called *Satellite Retrieval*. People often assume that experiential team-building activities are shared feats of sweat-inducing physical gamesmanship. While some games are indeed physical, many are about as exhausting as rocking in a rocking chair. The power of Satellite Retrieval doesn't come from shared physical triumph. No, the power lies in the activity's ability to create a pressure-filled environment in which the dysfunctional behaviors a group demonstrates at work are replicated in a harmless game with no lasting consequences for failure.

The goal of the activity is to help the group catch themselves being themselves. The activity works best if accompanied by a scenario customized to the needs of the group. In this case, a top-secret satellite, which contained the secret to strategic planning success, was falling back into Earth's atmosphere. The board was to build a retrieval device that would catch the satellite without breaking it. The satellite was actually an egg that was suspended 10 feet above the ground with some string, a hair net, and a bull clip. To build their retrieval device, the board was given a bag of material containing things like cotton balls, paper clips, paper cups, dental floss, tacks, coffee filters, straws. I instructed the board to divide into two groups: a design team and a construction team. Six members would be responsible for designing the retrieval device, the other six for constructing the device according to the exact specifications of the design team. Finally, I gave them a strict deadline of 20 minutes to build their device and catch the falling satellite.

As in the planning session, Percy's dominating personality came through. He personally selected which board members would be on each team, based on his assessment of who was a better thinker and who was a better doer. He himself would be on the design team because, as he jokingly said, "I am the only one I can trust to engineer this bloody thing right!" With the clock ticking, the board separated into the two groups. That's when Percy became an embellished version of himself. Every design idea offered by his fellow team members was shown by Percy to be flawed. There he was, a caricature of himself, shooting down everyone's ideas, rolling his eyes in frustration, using his facial expressions to transmit just how dumb he thought the group was. One by one, each member of the design team started to shut down until no one offered any more ideas. Exasperated and at his wit's end, Percy chided the team, telling them, "I'll just design the goddamn thing myself!"

The construction team was watching the ensuing dynamics in dismay. As Percy rummaged through the material bag with increasing desperation, they urged him to hurry up. Fifteen minutes had gone by and they would need the remaining time to build the device. Percy was trying to make sense of the materials as if they were pieces of a jigsaw puzzle, holding up each item and cocking it back and forth to see how it fit with the other items. *There must be some discernible logic to it,* he thought.

As the clock rounded 17 minutes both teams began pleading with him to stop slowing the process and move on. Desperate, Percy began scribbling out a design on the back of a coffee filter. Finally, at 18 minutes, he handed off his rumpled design to the construction team. They were livid. His scribbling was as complex as it was illegible. One construction team member crumpled the design into a little ball and tossed it in disgust at Percy's feet. With less than a minute left, Percy began furiously constructing the design himself as the other team members watched with their arms crossed. Without the benefit of anyone else's input, Percy had built a half-assed contraption that stood as a monument to his own arrogance. With 10 seconds left, one board member started counting down indifferently, "Ten, nine, eight, seven. . . ." As Percy squeezed the bull clip, the entire board watched in resignation as the egg missed the device entirely, smashing all over the ground.

The purpose of an experiential activity is never the activity itself—it is the dialogue that the activity provokes. Indeed, the real risks occur in the facilitated debrief because that's when the group becomes truly vulnerable. The Satellite Retrieval had brought a lot to the surface. As I gathered the board around me, it was clear from the looks on their faces that they were seething. After reminding them that it was just a game, I told them to be silent for 60 seconds.

Debriefing an activity that played out as harshly as this one has to be done with delicacy. Sometimes the best way to diffuse a group's anger and help them get some perspective is to give them a moment to regain their composure. The ensuing dialogue was among the richest I had ever facilitated. The board discussed how exasperated they had become with Percy in the game and how it reflected their feelings about him stifling the strategic planning process earlier in the day. They talked about how dejecting it felt when he shot down their ideas and how it caused them to check out. They talked about how frustrating it was never to be able to meet his standards and how his negativity permeated the atmosphere of the entire session. He took all the fun out of things.

All of the resentments that the board had stuffed down in the name of professional decorum had erupted to the surface through a simple game. When the purging was over, Percy, lips quivering, said softly, "I am so embarrassed." Few things are as disarming as an expression of humility. It was obvious to everyone that for Percy to have become this humble, the experience must have been tremendously humiliating. He went on to explain that he was just trying to prevent mistakes, and that it was hard for him to trust the group . . . or anyone else for that matter. He just wanted to be a good board member, someone who contributed to the safety and well-being of the organization. He noted how undeserving he had felt when he was selected for the board and how he had promised himself that he would do everything in his power to deserve this honor. Now he felt that he had failed them. Then, with his head bowed down, he told them that he would resign if they felt it would be in the best interest of the organization.

Percy had taken a risk. He had let the board see that the perfectionist was really just a man cloaking the burden of his imperfection. Slowly, the other board members began letting their guard down, adding how they too had contributed to the board's slow progress by enabling Percy's behavior and by acquiescing whenever he challenged their ideas. Some commented that they actually valued Percy's thoroughness and that they viewed him as a sentinel of the organization, protecting it from harm. No one wanted him to resign, just to ease up a bit and consider the input of the other board members. When they went back inside and resumed the strategic planning, it seemed as if a blockage had been removed from the way they connected with each other, and they were able to make substantial improvements to their strategic direction.

Being perfectly imperfect means recognizing that our control over outcomes has limits. If every outcome were controllable, if every mistake preventable, it wouldn't be a risk, it would be a certainty. Risk-taking involves chance and approximation. But more than that, it involves an encounter with our fallibility. Though our risks may indeed turn out perfectly, we as risk-takers will always have imperfections. Rather than, like Percy, being intolerant to imperfection, you should strive for excellence while also acknowledging the imperfect nature of risk, and the imperfect nature of yourself.

Getting Honest About Our Imperfections

For a lot of people, making a commitment to being perfectly imperfect is simply too hard to do because it means getting rigorously honest with yourself. This point is illustrated by the problem of alcoholism. One of the most commonly shared symptoms of alcoholism is denial. Alcoholics are notorious for engaging in all sorts of risky behavior while denying the existence of a drinking problem. I once had a friend whose drinking had caused him to bankrupt a business, demolish a new car, have his driver's license revoked, and ultimately destroy his marriage. Amidst all the wreckage, he could still look me square in the eyes and deny that he had a drinking problem, arguing, "Things could always be worse." Against overwhelming evidence to the contrary, alcoholics will deny the existence of a problem. What alcoholics deny is reality. As a rejection of reality, denial is a form of delusion that protects the alcoholic from the pain associated with assuming responsibility for the wreckage they have made of their lives.

Recovery for the alcoholic begins with an acknowledgment of his or her reality. It is no coincidence that the first of the twelve steps of Alcoholics Anonymous, the most successful treatment program for alcoholism, begins with two words: *We admitted.* These two words represent the end of denial and the beginning of reality acceptance. It is only after alcoholics can admit that they indeed *have* a problem, that they can begin to accept responsibility for dealing with it. As James Baldwin once said, "Not everything that is faced can be changed. But nothing can be changed until it is faced."

It is easy to see denial of reality in the extreme case of the alcoholic, but all people, to a greater or lesser degree, turn away from their imperfections, denying a sizeable piece of their own reality. Most of us prefer the safety of our denial to the uncomfortable exposure of our imperfections. We deny and repress our failings just so we can live with ourselves. But that which is repressed always rebels. When we deny our imperfections, we subconsciously strengthen their ability to direct and influence our lives. Propelled by the coiled spring of denial, the drinker binges, the brownnoser panders, the blamer condemns, and the controller oppresses. When it comes to our imperfections, they simply will not be denied.

Making the commitment to be perfectly imperfect is extremely difficult because it means facing the upsetting parts of your reality. Consider these upsetting questions:

- Are you a coward?

- Are you lazy?

- Are you stingy?

- Are you out of shape or overweight?

- Are you addicted to cigarettes?

- Are you prejudiced?

- Are you a bad spouse?

- Are you dominating?

- Are you defensive?

- Are you a blamer?

- Are you unhappy?

If you glanced over the list quickly, consider reading it again slowly. It is easy to turn away from such questions because they force you to consider your imperfections. Denial is an elaborate costume that by disguising our short-comings keeps us hidden from ourselves. But when we acknowledge only those aspects of ourselves that are pleasing, we remain incomplete in our level of self-awareness. Because it prevents us from developing a full and intimate relationship with ourselves, denial is a form of intimacy avoidance. A deep relationship with yourself, or anyone else for that matter, depends on taking the risk of self-disclosure. When you hide behind the mask of denial, your relationship to yourself remains shallow and insincere. Just as we are uncomfortable around people who are not genuine, when we deny the fullness of ourselves, warts and all, we grow uncomfortable with our own company. Denial is cowardice personified, and no one likes to hang around a coward . . . least of all when the coward is us.

Facing Yourself

Being perfectly imperfect means being rigorously honest. It means to stop denying or repressing your less-than-perfect parts, and to boldly face reality, in all its starkness. As the great American artist Walter Anderson once said, "Our lives improve only when we take chances—and the first and most difficult risk we can take is to be honest with ourselves."

The point of facing our imperfections is not to root them out so we can be perfect. Rather, we should acquaint ourselves with them, so that our self-knowledge is more complete. When we do this, we are better able to direct their influence over us, often converting them from sources of maladaptive behavior to a more adaptive kind. For example, ever since I was a kid, I've had a strong need for attention. I can remember when my parents had their friends over for cocktails, I would stand on my head (literally!) and sing *The*

Rain in Spain. It is really no surprise, then, that this need for attention would eventually translate into me becoming an exhibition high diver. Unlike polo, high diving is not a sport of kings, it is a sport of hotdogs.

Unfortunately, my need for attention turned me into a showoff. It always had to be about me. Finally, when I was 31, my live-in girlfriend walked out on me, explaining with exasperation, *I am tired of clapping for you.* Having already been through a failed relationship, it became obvious that I was part of the problem. But I was utterly clueless as to what to do about it. Heck, I didn't even know what *it* was. Broken-hearted and disenchanted, I finally sought therapy.

To enter therapy is to risk facing your imperfections. Through this process I was able to identify the reasons for my self-centeredness and to recognize how it had spilt over into every area of my life. Over time I learned how to accommodate my need for attention in more productive ways. Truthfully, I am still selfish and still have a strong need for attention. Now, however, I fulfill this need by allowing it to serve others. My profession affords me the opportunity to speak to large audiences. While I find addressing a room full of eager minds extremely gratifying, I believe my message about "purposeful risk-taking" benefits them also. My imperfect need for attention now serves both me and the people I address. And that is perfectly fine with me.

My story's happy ending is that after a five-year breakup, the woman who left me because she was tired of clapping is now my wife. Though she still claps a bit, I spend a lot more time clapping for her now too.

Be Perfectly Imperfect

I read somewhere that many great quilt makers like to sew an imperfect stitch among their patchwork. They do this as an act of homage—the idea being that only God has the right to be perfect. Imperfection provides a needed contrast for beauty to emerge so that it can be most appreciated. To be perfectly imperfect is to allow our imperfections to distinguish our more admirable qualities. Perhaps it is for this reason that, as my Grandmother used to say, "Everything God makes has a crack in it."

And how can you commit yourself to being perfectly imperfect? By replacing self-rejection with self-acceptance. By valuing your shortcomings for giving you your character, your quirkiness, and your humanness. By giving yourself a break and by recognizing that mistakes are not personal failings, but mile-markers on the winding road of progress. When you commit yourself to being perfectly imperfect, you come to appreciate risk-taking as a process of discovery, full of shortfalls and setbacks, but also full of serendipity and satisfaction. Being perfectly imperfect doesn't mean triumphing *over* our imperfections, it means triumphing *with* them.

Perfectionism: The Perfect Killjoy

A final thought about perfectionism. Perfectionism doesn't just inhibit our ability to take a risk, it inhibits our ability to *enjoy* it as well. Even risks that are deemed successful leave the perfectionist dissatisfied. Nobody's perfect, not even the perfectionist. And that presents an unsolvable riddle to them: you can't be satisfied unless you're perfect, and if true perfection is beyond our reach, then how can you ever be satisfied? Thus, perfectionism is ultimately joyless. To celebrate success would be to imply that they have reached a final plateau of satisfaction, a plateau of perfection. Since such a place cannot exist with finality, and since the perfectionist cannot stop striving until all things are perfect, stopping to celebrate would be an imperfect act. But hey, nobody's perfect.

Putting Principle 8 into Practice

✎   What things are you most perfectionistic about? How does your perfectionism serve you? How does it hurt you?

How do you view mistakes? How might this view impact how you feel about your current risk?

_____

_____

 Have you ever been accused of being "in denial"? What shortcomings do you have a hard time accepting about yourself? Why? What would you have to do to assimilate these imperfections instead of rejecting them?

_____

_____

 What about you is already "perfectly imperfect"? What needs to be?

_____

_____

 How might your perfectionism be getting in the way of being able to enjoy risk-taking?

_____

_____

Trespass
Continuously

> *"I am ashamed to think of how easily we capitulate to badges and names, to large societies and dead institutions."*
>
> —Ralph Waldo Emerson

> *"Wherever there is a man who exercises authority, there is a man who resists authority."*
>
> —Oscar Wilde

> *"Every great advance in natural knowledge has involved the absolute rejection of authority."*
>
> —Thomas Huxley

> *"Good behavior is the last refuge of mediocrity."*
>
> —Henry S. Haskins

Kurt Hahn was Adolph Hitler's first political prisoner.[1] In January 1933, one month after Hitler came to power, Hahn was jailed for openly challenging the Fuehrer's actions. Hahn was the founder of the Salem School, a school that focused on character development through the use of experiential education techniques. Upon learning that Hitler had sent a congratulatory telegram to five storm troopers who had murdered a young Communist by stomping him to death, Hahn had written a letter to all Salem alumni, telling those with ties to the SS to "terminate their allegiance either to Hitler or to Salem."[2] For thumbing his nose to Hitler, Hahn was imprisoned. He was released a few months later, but being of Jewish origin and having just had a foreshadow of Germany's future, Hahn fled to Great Britain. Within a year of arriving, he set up a new school in Scotland: The Gordonstoun School.

Like the earlier school, Gordonstoun used innovative, experiential approaches to education. Hahn believed that students benefit most when all aspects of their being are developed: mental, physical, emotional, and spiritual. Thus, the curriculum included rigorous study, strenuous exercise, periods of extended silence, craftwork, art and music, and character development. In addition to their studies, students learned mountain rescue techniques, participated in the local fire brigade, and rowed lifeboats along the rugged Scottish seacoast. Hahn believed that every student has a "grand passion" and saw it as his aim to help them shed the "misery of unimportance." He explained, "We are all better than we know; if only we can be brought to realize this, we might never settle for anything less."[3] The school became so successful that Britain's Prince Phillip, himself a Gordonstoun alumnus, insisted that each of his three sons, princes Charles, Andrew, and Edward, attend the school.

Living along the Scottish seacoast Hahn talked to many sailors who had been rescued after their ships were sunk by

German U-boats. Over time, he had noticed that for the stranded seamen the difference between survival and death often came down to willpower and attitude. He had seen many young and fit seamen die, while older and less fit ones lived. This observation prompted him to start a new life-training course, employing adventure-based education techniques to prepare people for dealing with all of life's toughest challenges. The goal of the new program was to train people to "not shirk from leadership" and to make independent decisions by putting "right action before expediency."[4]

Kurt Hahn is the founder of Outward Bound.

Today, Outward Bound is widely respected for helping people of all ages meet life's challenges by taking intelligent risks. But its early proponents met with stiff resistance when attempting to start the program in the United States. One of Hahn's American protégés, Josh Miner, wrote Hahn complaining that he had grown leery of trespassing on the domain of America's educational establishment.[5] Hahn's two-word reply represents an important way of demonstrating your commitment to your risk. It also forms the basis of our ninth Right Risk principle: *Trespass continuously*.

You Must Obey! . . . Sometimes

Progress demands obedience. From the Egyptian pyramids to the Great Wall of China, from the Eiffel Tower to the Apollo space program, no great work of humankind could have been achieved without obedience to a chain of command. Great collective deeds require the subjugation of personal interests to the "greater good." We are willing to postpone having our needs met when the benefits of doing so outweigh the benefits of getting what we want, or when following the desires of some authority preserves our communities. Organizations run most efficiently when people submit to a chain of command. Imagine, for example, conducting a military campaign without obedience? Or what if pilots flew self-directed without the uncompromising directives of an air traffic controller? Obedience is essential for social order, it keeps the group from becoming a mob. Hence our earliest lessons revolve around the importance of obedience. In the Bible, for example, two of the Ten Commandments deal directly with obedience to authority: *thou shalt have no gods before me* and *honor thy mother and thy father*. Further, it is by obeying all ten that we presumably get to heaven. Even the story of Abraham, where he obeys God's order to commit infanticide, reinforces the virtue of obedience.

But it doesn't take much imagination to recognize that obedience also has a sinister side. As social critic and novelist, C. P. Snow once wrote, "When you think of the long gloomy history of man, you will find more hideous crimes have been committed in the name of obedience than have ever been committed in the name of rebellion."[6] Unquestioned obedience to authority was, after all, at the black heart of Nazism, where the systematic slaughter of 6 million Jews, gypsies, mentally ill, and others was carried out by people who offered the uncomplicated rationale that they were simply "following orders." It may be easier for us to reconcile such atrocities as anomalies, fringe examples of human evil so rare as to seem remote from our own behavior. Surely we bear no resemblance to such diabolical souls.

But some disturbing research from the early 1970s showed that human obedience directed toward evil ends could not simply be explained away as a rare or a localized event. Moreover, the research also showed that the virtues of loyalty, discipline, and self-sacrifice (all of which obedience requires) could be twisted so as to bind even good souls to malevolent systems of authority. As unflattering as it may seem, under the right conditions, we, too, can be made to subjugate our own desires in order to carry out the evil orders of others.

Stanley Milgram's Shocking Study

Stanley Milgram was a Harvard-educated psychologist whose controversial book, *Obedience to Authority*, is considered a classic in the field of social psychology.[7] The book chronicles a series of experiments that Milgram conducted at Yale University during the 1960s and helps to explain how obedience acts as a forceful inhibitor of risk-taking. Here is how his study worked.

Imagine that you come across an ad in your local newspaper announcing a research study on the effects of punishment on learning. The announcement notes that participants will be paid a small fee for their time, no special training is needed, and they are seeking people from all walks of life. Hoping to make a quick buck, you sign up for the study. Upon entering the lab you meet the researcher and another person, a likeable middle-aged guy who is introduced as a recruit like yourself. The researcher, a stern, impassive fellow, explains that you and the other person will each have a distinct role in the experiment, one of you will be a "teacher" and the other a "learner." You each draw a piece of paper from a hat, and you find that yours says "teacher." You watch as the learner is strapped down to a chair and an electrode is pasted on his arm. The researcher says that the strap will help prevent "excessive movement," and that the electrode paste will keep the learner "from getting blisters and burns" during the experiment. After the learner expresses some concerns about his weak heart, the researcher tells him that though the shocks can be extremely painful, "they cause no permanent tissue damage."[8]

At this point you are led to an adjoining room that has an electronic console with some thirty switches, each labeled with a different voltage ranging from 15 to 450 volts and a verbal description ranging from "Slight shock" to "Danger, severe shock," to one ominously labeled "XXX" at the very end of the scale. You are to read from a list of word pairs and ask the learner to recite them back verbatim from memory, communicating through an intercom system. For each incorrect answer, you are to levy a shock in 15-volt increments. Just to make sure you are clear about the punishment you are to administer, you are given a sample shock of 45 volts. Yup, it's real, all right.

As you progress through the experiment, the learner makes a lot of mistakes requiring you to up the voltage of the punishment. Early on the learner doesn't seem to feel any pain. However, when you get to 75 volts he lets out an audible groan. At 120 volts, he says that the shocks are starting to hurt and reminds you about his heart condition. Troubled, you ask the experimenter for his advice, to which he passively replies, "The experiment requires that you go on." So you do.

At 150 volts, the learner shouts out, "Get me out of here!" Terrified, you tell the experimenter that you don't want to hurt the learner. He replies, "Whether the learner likes it or not, you must go on until he has learned all the word pairs correctly." After a few moments, you reluctantly proceed. At 300 volts, the learner vehemently protests that he refuses to answer any more questions. Incredulously, the experimenter tells you to treat the absence of an answer as an incorrect response and instructs you to punish accordingly. You feel trapped; the pressure building inside you is immense. You want to push your chair back and defiantly walk out of the room. But you just can't, you'll get in trouble for ruining the experiment. Reluctantly, you flip the switch to 315 volts, and the learner screams in agony. He screams even louder as you flip the switch to 330 volts. But at 345 volts, ominously, no more sounds are heard from the learner. You are petrified, worrying, *"Have I killed him?"* You plead for the experiment to stop, but you are told, "You have no other choice; you must go on." The pressure to disobey mounts; you feel fit to burst. The dilemma is maddening: disobey the experimenter and run the risk of ruining the study, or obey and run the risk of hurting—or even killing—the learner. What do you do?

If you are like most people, 66% in fact, you proceeded all the way to the maximum shock—the dreaded XXX switch—which you administered three times before the experiment was halted.[9] To your great relief, the learner was actually a confederate who, unbeknownst to you until after the experiment, received no shocks at all. As striking as it may seem, Milgram's study has been replicated over and over at numerous renowned universities throughout the world.[10] And though there are many variations of the study, the predominant goal is the same: to discover at what point a person will defy authority in the face of a clear moral imperative not to inflict harm.

The findings consistently show that people will subjugate their most ardently held moral values in order to obey the commands of an authority figure . . . even commands that could only be explained as evil. As Milgram notes, "The person who, with inner conviction, loathes stealing, killing, and assault may find himself performing these acts with relative ease when commanded by authority. Behavior that is unthinkable in an individual who is acting on his own may be executed without hesitation when carried out under orders."[11]

Notice how the pressure to disobey increased throughout the experiment. Milgram achieved this by using two mutually incompatible social pressures, the super-rational experimenter instructing you to proceed (pressure to obey) and the suffering victim begging you to stop (pressure to disobey). Through the antagonism created by these "counterforces," Milgram was looking for the point of rupture at which a person would switch from obedience to disobedience. Indeed, the specific voltage at which the participant refused to go any further signified the rupture point itself. But as noted, this switch was rarely made, and obedience was the predominant choice.

What is particularly remarkable is that the highest-level shocks were made in the absence of any real threat by the researcher. In fact, participants were told that they would receive their payment whether or not the study was successful. So the question becomes, why did most people continue shocking an innocent victim even after he begged them to stop? It turns out, for many of the same reasons people tend to obey those in authority: unwillingness to break a promise, belief in the legitimacy of the authority's credentials and directives, politeness, conflict avoidance, complete preoccupation with the task and inability to see the big picture, and fear of being "in trouble." When these forces are at play, we often divest ourselves of any personal accountability for our actions, becoming mere agents of the authority's power. Like echoes from the Nazi era, many participants in this experiment attributed responsibility for their actions to the authority figure, offering the age-old explanation that they were just "following orders."

I describe Milgram's study because it offers stark evidence of how our desire to obey inhibits us from taking risks. And just what is the inhibited risk in this experiment? This is important to clarify because it is easy to confuse the harmful acts of this experiment with the actual risk. The real risk in Milgram's study is not the act of inflicting pain on the learner. Doing exactly what you are told might describe allegiance, compliance, or even responsibility, but not risk. No, in these experiments, and indeed in many situations of obedience, the real risk is of disobedience, of trespassing beyond the authority's orders.

Disciplined Disobedience

Unlike in Milgram's study, in real life the consequences for disobeying authority can be quite real. As children we learn that disobeying our parents' wishes is the quickest way to a good spanking. Later, in adolescence, disobedient behavior may get us grounded. As we enter the work world, disobedience is seen as insubordination and is the surest way to getting fired. Hence, we devote an awful lot of time and energy to being well-behaved. Yet risk often requires just the opposite. Indeed, one of the most essential questions to ask yourself when facing a Right Risk is *who or what will I have to disobey in order to complete this risk?* Some risks require disobeying an actual person, like a boss, a parent, or a loved one. Others require disobeying institutions like our church or government. Most require disobeying your own fears, biases, and inclination not to risk. The point is, nearly every significant risk you will ever take is bound to offend someone, and the price of a Right Risk is often the stigma of misbehavior.

Right Risk involves self-leadership, the consequence of which is assuming responsibility for your own actions. In order to trespass beyond the "no" of someone in authority, you must be willing to say "yes" to your own authority. Then the orders you'll be following will be your own. At the same time, Right Risk involves self-followership because once you become your own authority, you also become responsible for following your directives. Thus making the commitment to trespass continuously involves both fierce independence and supreme obedience. It involves independently trespassing beyond the directives of an external authority, while being an obedient servant to the voice of our inner authority.

Right Versus Might

You are more likely to take a Right Risk when your moral convictions are stronger than your loyalty to those in authority. When this happens, as the following story illustrates, we are likely to choose trespassing over obeying.

On March 6, 1998, Hugh Thompson was awarded the Soldiers Medal at a ceremony at the Vietnam Veterans Memorial. Unlike most recipients of this coveted military award, Thompson didn't receive the award for obediently carrying out the orders of his commanding officers. To the contrary, he and his younger helicopter crewmates, Lawrence Coburn and Glenn Andreotta, won the award for defiantly landing their helicopter between American soldiers and their targets, the unarmed Vietnamese civilians in the tiny village of My Lai.[12]

The massacre at My Lai is perhaps the most shameful act in all of American military history. The American soldiers rounded up and killed some 500 defenseless Vietnamese civilians. The revelations were infuriating: women raped and mutilated, babies and elderly adults murdered. As young Army pilots, Thompson and his crewmates witnessed the carnage from the air. They tried to make sense of all of the dead bodies they saw piled in an irrigation ditch. Could our own soldiers have forced them into the ditch only to mow them down with machine guns? Thompson and his crew realized that this had gone well beyond the conventions of war. As Thompson put it, "I didn't want to be part of that. It wasn't war." Prodded by their own conscience and wanting to prevent further bloodshed, he and his team landed their chopper between their fellow troops and several elderly people and children who were being chased toward a shelter. After jumping out of the chopper and confronting the lieutenant leading the chase, Thompson decided to get the civilians out himself, instructing his crewmates to shoot any Americans who fired at the helpless victims, a command that would normally get one court-martialed. Though it took 30 years, Thompson and Coburn (Andreotta died in combat one month after the massacre) received their medals for choosing to defy military convention and to obey a higher authority than a chain of command: their own consciences.

Although the moral correctness of the actions of Thompson and his crewmates is beyond question, defying their chain of command must have been an extremely difficult act. Even in instances where the moral choice is less clear-cut, the decision to defy authority is anguishing. How are you to know, after all, whether your defiance is an act of courageous risk, or just arrogant insubordination? I suppose it has something to do with selflessness. Trespassing continuously—and for that matter Right Risk—does not mean perpetually having to get your way. *That* is arrogance. Instead, it means not bowing to others out of fear or convenience, particularly when their decisions will limit or harm others. Whether it was Kurt Hahn admonishing Hitler, or Josh Miner taking on the educational establishment to start Outward Bound in America, or the heroes who defied orders to save lives at My Lai, or the rare individuals who refused to administer shocks in Milgram's study, all of them were focused on serving others.

The Great Blasphemers

Bertrand Russell reportedly commented that all great ideas start out as blasphemy. I would add that all great deeds do as well. Defying authority, it turns out, is just as essential to human progress as obedience. History is filled with examples of people who trespassed continuously in order to bring about major scientific, cultural, and moral advancements.

Copernicus, Galileo, and Darwin defied the superstitions of the church; Gandhi defied the British government by marching to the Arabian sea and washing in the salt waters; Nelson Mandela defied South Africa's racist laws of apartheid; Cassius Clay (Muhammad Ali) defied the draft board; Rosa Parks defied a bus driver's order to give up her seat; Jeffery Wigand defied the unwritten rules of the tobacco fraternity; and the list goes on and on. Indeed, America herself was founded on acts of defiance. Let's not forget that nearly all of the Founding Fathers were *traitors* . . . to the British monarchy. Even Christianity would not exist had Christ surrendered to the Pharisees' rules instead of God's will. [Christ's scathing indictment of the Pharisees can be seen in the Gospel of Matthew (verse 23), where he calls them "blind fools," likening them to whitewashed tombs who are polished on the outside but rotten on the inside.] In each of these examples, the world would be an entirely different place had each person sheepishly "followed orders" and done exactly what they were told.

Each of us will face Pharisees in our lives. There will always be people who undermine our confidence, and who piously prop themselves up while holding us down. In many respects, the more "right" our risk, the more intensely the Pharisees will try to thwart our efforts. Thus the presence of Pharisees should bring a sense of relief to the Right Risktaker, a validation that they must be on to something good.

In the long run, right has might; good deeds overcome bad people. Making the commitment to trespass continuously means assuming responsibility for doing the right thing, regardless of who threatens or intimidates you. It means expecting that your Right Risk will incite detractors, and when it does, forging ahead anyway. Trespassing continuously means being owned by no one, while serving everyone.

Saintly Rebels

In *The Courage to Create,* Rollo May points out that throughout history the saint and the rebel very often have been the same person.[13] People like Jesus, Gandhi, Socrates, and Joan of Arc possessed a wonderful blend of virtue and verve. They were willing—and in some cases eager—to trespass continuously on the province of the oppressive guardians of the status quo. As these saintly rebels showed us, Right Risks involve mixing moral decency with unruly indignation. It was through their disobedience to secular authorities that they were most able to demonstrate their allegiance to a higher one: a God of their understanding.

Putting Principle 9 into Practice

🖎 How has being obedient caused you to avoid risks in
   the past? In what instances do you use "following
   orders" as an excuse for abdicating responsibility?

   _____

   _____

🖎 What acts of disobedience are you most proud of?
   Least proud of?

   _____

   _____

🖎 Who or what will you have to disobey to complete
   your big risk? How big a barrier is this toward taking
   your risk?

   _____

   _____

🖎 Who is your favorite "saintly rebel"? Why?

   _____

   _____

🖎 What are some of your convictions or moral rules?
   How far would you go in challenging authority to
   uphold them?

   _____

   _____

Expose
Yourself

❋

"The soul wants to be attached, involved, and even struck, because it is through such intimacy that it is nourished, initiated, and deepened."

—Thomas Moore, SoulMates

Like a lot of men, my relationship with my father is complex. Over the years it has moved from love, to hate, to love again. When I was a boy, he was the hero of the household, leaving to conquer the world each morning, and sitting at the head of the dinner table each night. But as I moved into adolescence, and then into my young twenties, we argued a lot. The problem was, we were similar people looking at the world in different ways; he with jaded cynicism, me with rose-colored glasses. I resented him for always dousing my idealistic optimism for a better world with resigned pessimism for a worse one. *He was no hero*, I thought, *just a bitter curmudgeon who'd let life beat him down.*

As my resentments toward my father deepened, I wrote him off. Though I had moved away from home to become a high diving gypsy at 21, I often stayed in close contact with the rest of my family through cards, letters, and occasional phone calls. But I purposely left him out. *He is a bad father,* I told myself, *so I will be a bad son.*

In 1991, my grandfather was diagnosed with cancer. He had been diagnosed with Alzheimer's some time earlier. My father had become, in effect, a father to his father. My grandfather had been my father's hero, and with his death approaching, my father began to reflect on the importance of the father/son bond. He became bothered by the distance that had grown between us. At the same time, I had begun to wonder how I would feel if my father died. I honestly didn't know if I would miss him, but I was 100% sure that I would mourn the loss of the *potential* of what could have been. If my father died, I didn't want to shake my head and say, *what a shame we didn't work things out.* As my grandfather's condition worsened, I decided to fly home to say my goodbyes.

My father and I wanted more of our relationship, but neither of us knew how to ask for it. Toward the end of my visit, we decided to go for a hike not far from where my father grew up. Half way through our hike, my father made the first move, saying, "I notice that you don't call or write me. You seem to have written me off." His words weren't antagonistic, as they'd often been in the past, rather they were tinged with hurt. His tone suggested that he thought I was somehow embarrassed of him. I was taken back by his openness, but also relieved. Slowly I began to open up to him about some of the resentments that I'd been carrying for a long time. I was shaking. Even at 31, I was afraid of his temper. A temper that was matched only by . . . well . . . my own.

As we hiked along, I knew that we were in the midst of a high-stakes conversation. In opening up to one another, we stood the chance of further severing, and perhaps ending, our relationship. But I also knew that we were in a different place now. My grandfather's pending death opened up a space of mutual yearning between my father and me. After saying my peace, I startled even myself, telling him, "I want you to know that I love you, Dad, and I want us to be closer."

Underneath our resentments lies anger, and underneath our anger lies hurt, and underneath our hurt lies love. After walking a while in silence, my father stopped in his tracks, looked me in the eyes and said, "I love you too, Billy, let's do better."

I can honestly say that that was one of the riskiest, and most important conversations I ever had. It dramatically altered the course of our relationship. By putting down our barriers we were able to connect in a new way. The conversation helped me stop holding my Dad up to heroic, and unattainable, expectations. It helped me begin to see my Dad as a man with flaws, like me, but as someone who worked really hard to make a better life for our family. Our conversation helped give us a new foundation on which our relationship could grow—our newly affirmed love for each other. But here is the point, none of this would have happened had we not first took the risk of revealing ourselves to each other. Since then I have committed myself to Right Risk Principle 10: *Expose yourself.*

The Risk of Exposure

Risk-taking is, by definition, being *exposed* to harm. The predominant feeling elicited by being exposed to risk is vulnerability, and life's most vulnerable moments are not when peering over the edge of a cliff but looking someone squarely in the eye. I am convinced that exposing our true selves to a boss, a coworker, a parent, or a loved one, takes more courage than performing a 100-foot high dive. Interpersonal risks are extremely scary because they are less controllable than risks of a more concrete nature. When performing a high dive, for example, one can predict with 100% accuracy that one will always go down. When revealing your true feelings to another human being, however, all bets are off as to how he or she will react. People, as emotional beings, are volatile. The slightest comment can set us off and trigger our emotions. At one time or another, each of us has had to tiptoe around the emotions of someone else. And at one time or another, someone has tiptoed around ours as well.

A friend of mine used to tell me that *a broken spirit is far worse than a broken bone.* When we expose our emotional selves we stand the chance of getting hurt deeply and permanently. But the rub is, you can't build trust, and therefore you can't build enduring relationships, without first taking the risk of opening yourselves up to one another. Indeed, the depth of the trust between two people is often a function of the emotional high dives they've been willing to take together.

Committing to the principle of exposing yourself means to accept the inherent risks that accompany personal disclosure. In many respects, to apply this principle is to validate that you are fully committed to all the other principles. Exposing yourself means going beyond just committing to a given risk as a one-time event, and committing yourself to risk-taking as a way of interacting with the world. Stretching your comfort zones is not enough; you must learn to live outside of them entirely, in a way that accepts vulnerability as an essential part of the human condition.

Comfort, in the context of comfort zone, is just a euphemism for fear. When your life is encased in tightly defined zones of comfort, you are a person whose life is restricted by fear. But when you burst through your comfort zones, and allow yourself to be wonderfully exposed, you become a person with an enlarged capacity to take risks in every area of your life, even life's more intimate parts. Being an exposed person means more than just taking physical, intellectual, or creative risks. It means applying the Right Risk principles in the areas where your risks are most consequential: your relationships. Exposing yourself means opening your arms to taking interpersonal risks.

Avoiding the Clash

The raw feelings that come with emotional risk-taking can cause acute risk aversion, especially when the emotional risk involves interpersonal conflict. Yet by avoiding conflict, and remaining emotionally concealed, we stunt our maturity, weaken our confidence, and erode our relationships. Indeed, as related in the incident below, in extreme instances, failing to expose your true thoughts and feelings can even result in physical injury.

In 1988, I was named team captain of our diving show in Seattle, Washington. This was our first time performing at this amusement park, so I was very conscious of the need to impress the client quickly.

The first show of the season was always special, particularly in the case of an inaugural season at a new park. Like any other business, the idea was to deliver a top-notch product so that you would please the customer and thereby extend the contract. The first show was our chance to make a good first impression with the park management. Accordingly, we always aimed to launch the opening show with a "splash." For this reason, the president of our company, Don Jewel, decided to fly up from Los Angeles and join the performance.[1] Don was a legend in the high-diving business. He founded the company with money he had received for performing a world-record high dive (168 feet) into Baltimore Harbor in 1981. Don reasoned that by coming to Seattle and promoting the opportunity to see a former world-record holder perform, he could draw more local press to the show.

While Don's reasoning was sound, his perception of reality was flawed. Though Don was indeed a former world-record holder, his record dive had nearly cost him his life. Don wasn't a diver; he was a wrestler. In front of a nationally televised audience, while traveling at speeds approaching terminal velocity, Don had crashed into Baltimore Harbor hunched over like a caveman. He was barely able to get out of the water—a requisite for being awarded the record. While the crew in Seattle was curious to see Don dive again, I had serious misgivings. In the eight years since his big dive, Don had gained nearly 70 pounds! Worse still, he had done only a handful of dives since breaking the world record eight years earlier.

One of the fundamental laws of risk-taking is to soberly assess reality. The reality was, there was no way in hell that Don should be doing this dive. Recognizing the gravity of the situation, but not wanting to offend Don, I casually suggested that he let me or one of the other divers do the dive. He refused, and even though I *knew* that this was madness, I didn't protest. Like his world-record debacle, this dive would be taken in a militant state of delusion.

The flailing arms and legs were the first signs that something was wrong. From 100 feet a small outward jump of only a few feet can end up carrying you 20 feet out by the time you strike the water. Don had leapt off the platform at full throttle and was traveling out far past the middle of the pool. It was clear from his wild gesticulations that he was well aware that he was in trouble. The other divers and I could see instantly that Don was off-kilter. Our cocky all-American smiles turned to expressions of utter terror. Some of us had extended our hands toward Don as if we could somehow telepathically *will* him back into control. Even the audience could tell there was something wrong. Don was heading for the edge of the pool rotating past vertical and kicking his legs. He looked like someone who had tipped too far back in his chair while having a seizure. As if to accentuate the absurdity of the moment, Don blurted out a fully audible "shit!" just as he crashed into the pool drenching the audience with a huge plume of water.

For a moment we were all stunned. Then Don hoisted himself out of the pool, mustered a sheepish wave to the audience, and scurried backstage. When the rest of us joined him, Don was lying on the ground in the fetal position. All he could say was "Get an ambulance."

Don had indeed made a splash. He was wheeled out of the park on a stretcher, in full view of everyone. He would spend the next three days cloistered at a Seattle hospital recuperating from a broken back. Don had fractured three vertebrae in his lower lumbar region. This time there was no world record to show for his spectacle. He did, however, get to wear a girdle for a couple of months.

This story illustrates the dangers that can arise when we conceal our true feelings to protect the feelings of others. It also shows what happens when overconfidence collides with underconfidence. Don's headstrong ego had poisoned his judgment and he had become oblivious to the dangers of his risk. He was defiantly "disrespecting the ladder" and provoking the risk gods. But Don's fearlessness was offset by my fearfulness. I was so afraid of confronting Don, so afraid of pissing him off, and so afraid of hurting his feelings that I let him walk into a life-threatening situation. While Don was guilty of arrogance, I was guilty of avoidance. My lack of assertion in confronting Don made me feel culpable for his fractured back. My fear of injuring his feelings had resulted in his physically injuring his body. Instead of exposing my true misgivings in an assertive way, I allowed Don's conviction to trump my courage. Not only did I have a responsibility to confront him as a friend, but I had a responsibility to do so as the team captain as well. Instead, personally and professionally, I failed him.

Staying Under Cover

Committing to the principle of exposing yourself means carrying the other Right Risk principles into every area of your life. Perhaps the riskiest place to apply this principle is in our worklives. When it comes to exposing our true selves at work, most of us prefer to remain under cover. Of course our organizations largely promote this behavior. For example, while most organizations have mechanisms for downward feedback in the form of performance appraisals and reviews, upward feedback is mostly a frozen pipeline. With a straight face, one executive was so bold as to tell me that upward feedback (such as 360-degree feedback) is dangerous because it promotes "leadership insecurity" and undermines corporate discipline. In a sense, he was saying that to remain bastions of social control, the last thing we want is for the troops to let the emperors know when they're naked. This exec can take solace in the fact that upward feedback is as rare as secure leadership. Ask yourself, when was the last time you exposed yourself by giving your boss a performance review?

It is odd that behavior we would not tolerate outside of work often goes unaddressed inside of work, particularly in the upper echelons. The designation "boss," and the power derived from the title, seems to entitle the boss to a higher degree of behavioral latitude. Higher-ups are allowed to get away with behavior that is not tolerated at lower levels. The higher the hierarchical altitude, the more impatience, turfism, moodiness, pettiness, and abrasiveness. Social dominance is a function of ego, and the game of organizational leapfrog often equates to survival of the scariest. When everyone is afraid of you, you don't have to deal with them . . . they have to deal with you. Those brave souls who expose themselves by questioning the behavior or decisions of scary executives do so at their own peril. Yet nowhere is unfiltered feedback more needed than at the upper echelons. Without it, executives become in danger of rendering decisions that may satisfy the interest of their egos but undermine the interests of their businesses.

Expecting people to expose their true opinions to a lousy boss may seem unrealistic. The reality is that people get fired for exposing themselves at work. Besides, tolerating a bad boss keeps the paychecks rolling in and puts food on the table. All of this is true, of course. But without these realities to contend with, exposing yourself wouldn't be a risk. The fact that there *is* a possibility of reprisal is what makes it risk.

There are two problems with failing to take the risk of exposing your opinions to a bad boss—one affects the boss, and the other affects the employee. First, we allow their corrosive behavior to continue or worsen, undermining employee morale. Second, we compromise our principles, weakening both our resolve and our stature within the company. Remaining under cover is, essentially, a sin of omission—failing to do what we ought to do. Over time, we may get a reputation as being a pushover or a lackey, the death knell for any aspiring career.

A Diver Exposed

I rely upon my own experience in drawing these conclusions about the merits of exposing yourself at work. As a young, insecure leader, I once received some hard-hitting feedback from one of my divers. In 1986, after only two years of performing, I was asked to lead our team at WaterCountry USA in Williamsburg, Virginia. I had learned from my previous team captains that it is important to spend a lot of time critiquing the diver's performance early on in the season, so I rode the team hard in the weeks leading up to the first day of shows. Being only 23 and not wanting to seem weak in front of the older divers, after each show I would stride backstage like General Patton and grill the team. One day after coming down hard on the team for a sloppy performance, I dismissed them in utter disgust. One diver, however, lingered behind. Steve Willard was one of our most talented performers. When the other divers were out of earshot, Steve stood in front of me and said, "Listen, Treasurer, who do you think you are? Where do you get off talking to us like that? Do you think that by berating us and being rude, that you will earn our respect? All you do is harp on our mistakes. What are you trying to do, make us afraid of you? If you talk to us like that again, I'll walk."

At first, Steve's words ticked me off. *How dare he talk back to me like that! I'm his boss! I'll fire his ass!* I thought. But the more I internalized it, the more I knew he had taken a risk, and that he was right. I wasn't being a leader, I was being a jerk. The phrase that caught my attention the most was "Who do you think you are?" Clearly, I was not being myself. Instead, I had constructed a bastardized leadership style based on all the bosses who had ever led me. I was me being them. I was a phony.

To his credit, Steve had exposed his true feelings to me and in the process did, in fact, cause me to become more insecure—temporarily. Steve's feedback set off a chain of events that would ultimately change my life. His words prompted me to become intensely interested in learning about leadership, influence, and motivation. I started reading books on team dynamics. Eventually, this interest would carry me to graduate school where I would write my masters thesis on motivational leadership. Unwittingly, Steve had awakened a calling in me. Even today, as the head of a company that helps people take risks, I benefit from the risk that Steve took by exposing himself to me.

Exposing the Truth

The principle of exposing ourselves is fundamentally about honesty. As much as we all know the virtues of honesty, we seem to have a hard time putting it into practice, opting instead for socially appropriate lying. Lying comes easier than the truth for two reasons. First, it keeps us from hurting each other's feelings. Second, it helps us avoid conflict. So, when a wife asks a husband, "Do I look fat?" and a husband asks a wife, "Is my bald spot getting bigger?" both reply, "Of course not, dear!" . . . even if it is not the truth.

To expose yourself often requires confronting others with your truth, not to admonish or inflict pain, but to foster growth. For example, early in my career, my mentor told me that I was a brownnoser. He didn't try to sugarcoat it or protect my feelings; he just looked me square in the eye and stated it. Afterwards, he just sat there and let me deal with my own emotions. He was responsible for the feedback, I was responsible for the feelings. The moment was very awkward but very necessary. It forced me to consider the need to change. By the time I left his office, I was actually in a good mood. He had closed a blind spot by offering me a few specific examples and then providing me with sound advice for future growth.

Personal growth would be next to impossible without the type of unvarnished feedback that my mentor gave me. Think about your own growth. Hasn't it come to you mostly as a result of someone exposing *their* truth about *your* blind spot?

Leaving the Harbor of Resentments

One of the major benefits of exposing ourselves is that it prevents resentments from growing. Resentments are the number one reason for poor relationships between people. We get resentful about lots of things, such as favoritism, unfairness, not being appreciated, not getting our way, other people's success, etc. But most commonly we get resentful when someone says something hurtful to us and instead of addressing it straight away, we swallow it.

Unaddressed resentments are like lead ornaments that hang inside us weighing us down. Because we are the ones holding the grudge, the person we are resenting may have no idea that anything is wrong and thus can't remedy the situation. Or they know something is wrong because we transmit it to them through our moody or curt behavior, but because we don't actually tell them, they are left to guess what is the matter. Even in this case, we carry the burden of resentment, at them and at ourselves for not telling them.

Though emotional volatility makes disclosing resentments risky, the risks of unaddressed resentments are greater. I have seen resentments fester to the point where they have caused people to quit jobs, break off friendships, boycott family reunions, and end marriages. I know a brother and sister who didn't talk for eight years because of resentments they held toward each other.

What surprises me is the sheer amount of time spent carrying the resentment when the act of disclosing them is often very brief. We may spend weeks imagining arguments with the other person, anguishing over what we'd like to tell them. But when we actually muster up the courage to confront the issue, resolution, one way or the other, occurs very quickly. Knowing this, my advice to coachees who are harboring resentments is to expose them swiftly in order to strengthen their chances of keeping their relationships healthy and vibrant.

Don't Get So Close to Me

One of the main reasons we avoid exposing ourselves is fear of intimacy. When we reveal ourselves to someone else, we stand a very real chance of deepening our relationship, and, therefore, becoming more intimate with each other. According to Thomas Moore, the author of *Soul Mates*, the word *intimacy* means "profound interior."[2] It comes from the Latin *inter* meaning "within" and can also be translated as "most within" or "within-est." In taking emotional risks with each other, we reveal those portions of ourselves that normally remain ensconced within our psychological interior.

As emotional risk, intimacy is a double-edged sword. First, in revealing our emotions, we unmask a truer, more authentic version of ourselves. Disrobed of image and pretense, we stand emotionally naked. The danger of being revealed this way is that we are vulnerable to being rejected, and as a rejection of our truest self, this is a rejection of the worst kind. For some, however, the second danger is more threatening: In exposing our true selves we might be accepted to the point of obligation. In revealing ourselves we run a very real risk of building closer connections with people. The more we bond, the more likely it is that we will take an interest in them and become more sensitive to their needs. Eventually we may even grow to care about them and will no longer be able to dismiss or ignore them. The more intimate our relationship becomes, the more difficult it is to extricate ourselves from the obligations of friendship and to preserve our independence. Fears of intimacy are fears of dependence, responsibility, confinement, and obligation.

Exposing yourself takes real courage because it means becoming more emotionally available and engaged. When we are emotionally present, we listen with greater intensity, we are less reluctant to expose our vulnerabilities, we are more attuned to the needs of others, and we are more willing to work through relationship-straining confrontations. To be emotionally engaged means living in a more openhearted, sincere, and exposed way. Yes, living this way means we will suffer through rejections. And, yes, it also means that we will occasionally feel smothered under the obligation of friendship. As Moore says, "The courage required to open one's soul to express itself or receive another is infinitely more demanding than the efforts we put into avoidance of intimacy."[3] Over time, though, the emotionally engaged person learns to accommodate both the need to preserve one's independence and the need to form deeper, and ultimately more durable relationships.

Overexposure

There is always the danger, of course, in being overexposed. All of us know people who seem to have lost all sense of privacy or diplomacy. But the principle of exposure is not about having no emotional or interpersonal boundaries. Instead it is about recognizing that all risk involves exposure, and therefore vulnerability. In the same way we expose our money, bodies, and brains to take financial, physical, and intellectual risks, we must expose our feelings to take emotional risks. Exposing yourself means having no hidden agendas, and living in an open, nonmanipulative way. Not in a way that betrays our privacy, but in a way that affirms our character.

Putting Principle 10 into Practice

Think of a time when you took the risk of exposing your true feelings to someone else. What was the issue that you were confronting? What was the outcome? Did exposing yourself make things better or worse?

_____

_____

In what ways do you avoid exposing your true thoughts, feelings, and opinions? In these instances, why is remaining under cover easier than exposing yourself?

What interpersonal risk have you been avoiding? Why? What would it take for you to confront the issue? How might exposing yourself benefit the relationship?

On a piece of paper, draw a picture of the "lead weight" resentments that you may be carrying around. Use circles to illustrate their size. How many lead weights are you carrying? How are they getting in the way of your relationships? How can you remove them?

Are you comfortable taking emotional risks or do they scare you? Why? What would it take for you to become more emotionally revealed?

Part Five

Reaping the Rewards of Right Risk

Warning: Proceed with Caution!!!

You are about to enter the most dangerous part of the entire book—it is more provocative, more forceful, and more opinionated than all those preceding. This chapter deals with the truth. My truth. The truth as I see it. I won't mince words and I don't intend to coddle. The truth doesn't aim to please, it aims to reveal—which can be both painful and liberating. Yes, the truth sets us free, but what it frees us from are often deeply rooted ways of thinking that have become at once familiar, comfortable . . . and limiting.

Before you begin, I need to make two additional points. First, as much as I wrote this book for you, the reader, I also wrote it for me, a flawed man. I am a person who, in too many instances, has compromised myself in order to obey people I neither respected nor agreed with. In big ways and in small, I have been true to others at the expense of being true to myself. I have been well behaved . . . but pacing. This part reflects the book's most personal aim: to speak my truth.

Second, the decision about whether or not to read this rests entirely with you. I would ask, however, that you consider whether or not you have found the book valuable thus far. The question is, *do you trust me?* If so, then I invite you to demonstrate that trust by turning the page and reading on. If not, then please recall that in the beginning of the book I told you that I would be asking you to take a risk. According to Peter L. Bernstein, author of *Against the Gods: The Remarkable Story of Risk*, the oldest definition of the word risk comes from the Latin *riscaré*, which means "to dare." Thus, in the truest sense of the words, I *dare* you to enter this final part.

The Rightest
Risk of All

"*How in heaven's name are you going to find your own track if you are always doing what society tells you?*"

—Joseph Campbell

"*There is a road, no simple highway*
Between the dawn and the dark of night.
And if you go no one may follow
That path is for your steps alone."

—The Grateful Dead, *"Ripple"*

Physician Heal Thyself

Bill Treasurer is a fake! I came to that conclusion about a year after I had become a full-time internal executive coach at Accenture. The role itself was perfect. I had a budget, a good deal of latitude to do the job as I saw fit, and although most of my coachees outranked me, all had signed an agreement that it would be a "levelless" relationship. Besides all that, I was making a lot of money doing what I love to do, helping people grow.

Why was I a fake? Because the more I coached my clients, the more I realized that my own beliefs and actions were out of step. As a coach, it is my job to help *accentuate* my coachees, to help them become the person they want to become. To do this, I help coachees identify their deepest aspirations, and then help them create a plan for making those aspirations real. While I was successful in helping my coachees apply these techniques, I wasn't applying them in my own life. I had become the consultant's consultant, someone who could give advice better than he could apply it.

The problem was, I was not being the person I wanted to become. I was living an inauthentic life.

The Risks of Being Yourself

Throughout the ages, the most consistent prescription for personal well-being is this: *Be who you must be.* The Greek poet Pindar said, "Grow into what you are." Ralph Waldo Emerson said, "Insist on yourself, never imitate." Famed psychologist Erich Fromm said, "Man's main task in life is to give birth to himself, to become what he potentially is." Robert Louis Stevenson said, "To be what we are, and to become what we are capable of becoming, is the only end in life." And Abraham Maslow said, "A musician must make music, an artist must paint, a poet must write if he is to be ultimately at peace with himself. What a man can be, he must be."[1]

These sages said explicitly what we all know implicitly, that when you have become far removed from who you are supposed to be, when your work-self and personal-self are wholly different people, and when the masks you wear don't look anything like your real face, you expend too much energy living a life of pretense.

Authenticity has to do with integrity. When the person we portray to the world is the same as the person we truly are, we are being our authentic self. When we are authentic, *we are who we are*, take us or leave us. To live authentically is to live without pretense, and to express and assert the gift of your individuality. Living authentically means being psychologically patriotic, proud of who you are. The benefit of being our authentic selves is that instead of wasting time pretending to be someone we are not, we have more impassioned energy to get on with the business of living. Living a life of authenticity represents the end to an exhausting game of make-believe.

Shake the Global Village

At no time in the history of the world has the need for us to *be who we must be* been greater. As the world's communications infrastructure turns us into a "global village," there is a danger of creating mass homogeneity. People in developing countries are watching reruns of *Gilligan's Island*. Kids in Asian slums show how cool they are by wearing Nike sneakers. You can find the "golden arches" in over 120 countries.

Yvon Chouinard, the irrepressible founder of Patagonia, a brand of pricey outdoor clothes, summed up the dangers of sameness when he said, "I knew Man was doomed when I realized that his strongest inclination was toward ever-increasing homogeneity—which goes completely against the grain of Nature. Nature moves toward ever-increasing diversity. Diversity is Nature's strength."[2] Chouinard's comments are as accurate as they are ironic; Patagonia used to connote that remote land at the edge of the world, now it connotes stylish fleece pullovers for trendy suburbanites.

The danger of our growing homogeneity is that the individual becomes swallowed up by the collective, diluting the potency of everyone. When our identities are subsumed by the masses, our uniqueness is stripped, our sense of self is lost, and our dignity erodes. We become passively disengaged and collectively indifferent. Perhaps no phrase epitomizes today's growing indifference as much as this: "whatever."

Cultures that adopt a "whatever" philosophy—Whatever Societies—lack depth of character. Whatever Societies are places where distinctions between people are made not by who they *are*, but by what they *have*. In Whatever Societies, *getting* is more important than *giving*, because getting is how one distinguishes oneself. People here are judged not by one's character on the inside, but by the garnishes on the outside; what they wear, what they drive, and where they live. In Whatever Societies identities are forged through acquisition; the more *I have*, the more *I am*. Therefore, if people aren't *buying*, they aren't *being*. The entire economic engine, indeed the entire purpose of such societies, is based on appetite. In Whatever Societies, your most important duty is to be a good consumer, because consumption makes the whole thing work.

The problem with Whatever Societies is that they are made up of people with no identity of their own. People with all the originality of a prefab subdivision. People who chose their hairstyles, their clothes, and the names of their children based on popular sitcom characters. People who, in their professional lives, are more concerned with "branding" themselves, than *being* themselves.

Other than material acquisition, Whatever Societies stand for nothing in particular. As long as one's bank account is fat, no one really cares about the political climate, environmental situation, or state of the outside world. Prosperity anesthetizes, and the richer a Whatever Society gets, the more it chooses consumption over compassion, greed over generosity, and selfishness over selflessness. People take the wrong risks for the wrong reasons, risks that feed the ego but fail to nourish the heart. In such places the only risks worth taking are the shallow ones, the ones that promise to make a person wealthy, powerful, or famous. Otherwise, why bother endangering yourself?

Loitering at the Gates of Hell

In *The Divine Comedy* of Dante (Vol. I: *Inferno*), a haunting image provides a stark warning for people who adopt a Whatever philosophy, and in the process reinforces the merits of *being who one must be*. Dante's *Inferno*, you will recall, tells the story of a man who midway through his life realizes that the person he has become and the person he wanted to be are two wholly different people. To get from where he is (his compromised self) to where he wants to be (his true self), Dante must travel through the depths of hell. Just before embarking on his journey, he notices a group of people loitering outside the gates of hell. They are the souls who heaven didn't want and hell wouldn't have.

As Dante describes it, "Heaven, to keep its beauty, cast them out, but even hell itself would not receive them . . . " Just who are these pathetic souls? They are the people who did nothing meritorious or reprehensible, earning neither blame nor praise, and who, consequently, in Dante's words, "never truly lived."[3] They are the people who never *stood* for anything, benign people, diluted and impotent people, people who led irrelevant lives . . . Whatever People. And what is the punishment for the rejects of both heaven and hell? To march aimlessly behind an empty banner that signifies nothing. For just as these souls stood for nothing in life, they will stand for nothing in eternity as well.

The Danger of Being Ourselves

What about you? Are you a Whatever Person? Would you know if you were? Ask yourself these tough questions:

- Are you living a lie?

- Does your life stand for anything? What?

- Are you selling out in some area of your life? Have slow, incremental compromises turned you into the person you never wanted to be?

- Would the person you are at work be welcomed into your home?

- Do you judge others mainly by their appearances?

- Does your life revolve around money? Which of these do you equate it with: freedom, happiness, security, status, and/or power?

- Would people describe you as "genuine," "real," or "down to earth"? Are you?

- Is your true self the self that the world gets to see?

- Are you the person that you always wanted to become?

If you are disappointed with your answers, take heart. *Whatever* does not have to be *forever*. Like Dante, it is never too late to save your life. But, like Dante, to become the person you are supposed to become, you may have to go through hell to get there. Why? Because being our authentic selves is a huge risk. If it wasn't, it would be a more universally pursued goal. But authenticity is more than a risk, it is the Rightest Risk of all. Authenticity is a life imperative, because to live a compromised life is to live a life of irrelevance. Life's journey should be one of self-discovery, not self-rejection.

The best use of the 10 Right Risk principles is to use them to reclaim your identity, to take the risk of being yourself. But make no mistake, there are hazards along the way. Consider some of the risks of being authentic:

Being authentic means assuming full responsibility for your own life

Emerson once wrote, "Society everywhere is in a conspiracy against the personhood of its members . . . The virtue in most request is conformity."[4] Conformity is easy because all it requires is abdication. When we conform, we allow society to tell us what to think, what to believe, what to value, and even what to wear. The authentic person rejects the notion that society always knows best. She refuses to rely on society to provide all her answers, to set all her rules, to determine her worth, to make up her mind. She spends a lot more time governing her own thoughts and actions. Authenticity requires responsibility. The authentic person forms her own opinions, makes her own choices, and, therefore, assumes responsibility for making her own mistakes.

Being authentic prompts resentment

When *you are who you are* and not as society would have you be, you become a butterfly among a bunch of caterpillars. You stand out. As the full plumage of the authentic person's originality unfurls, she burns bright with fresh ideas. Her individuality contrasts the conformity of everyone else, making it more pronounced. This brings new dangers. *What gives her the right to think that way?* society asks. Like a plantation master seeing a former slave, society resents the authentic person's newfound freedom. The authentic person has grown more powerful and independent; she is far less intimidated by society's discipline, far less dependent upon society's permission or approval, and far less subservient to society's authority. She doesn't always do what society insists. She is, in society's view, out of control. And the first instinct of the controller is to control the uncontrolled.

Being authentic requires self-acceptance

At its base, being authentic means being truthful. The authentic person knows that to be fully authenticated, she must be able to accept and integrate her beauty *and* her ugliness. One is needed to contrast the other. The authentic person isn't afraid to acquaint herself with her less-than-perfect side. Personal fidelity, that defining characteristic of the authentic person, demands being faithful to the totality of yourself, even your less desirable parts.

❁

Keep in mind that being authentic is not about being different. All of us have seen those counterculturalists whose very difference is based on conformity. In their desire to be different they clump together in groups of *sameness*. "Phisheads," "Granolaheads," "Goths," and the pierced-everything crowd fall into this category. For the authentic person, being different is far less important than being *real*. Being authentic means saying, "I am somebody"—not because of how I look, what I own, or where I live, but because of the genuineness and distinctiveness of my character.

The High-Diving Hypocrite

I know what it is like to be a sell-out. I know what it is like to parcel out large portions of your soul to have a comfortable, but compromised, life. I have faced situations of consequence and allowed my decision to be a decidedly uncommitted "Whatever." As I mentioned at the start of the chapter, though I was a successful coach, I was a fake. I was a coach who advised one thing, but applied another. I was a man hiding from himself.

Good coaching is essentially about helping people become their authentic selves. For me, I knew down deep that I wanted to be a writer, professional speaker, and independent consultant . . . in that order. But I knew that to be this person, I would have to take a giant leap with my life. Let me tell you, there is a great deal of security in a steady paycheck. Besides that, having been at Accenture for almost six years, I was well networked and established. So, I buried my dreams under heaps of reality, and told myself to be more practical.

The problem with buried dreams is that they make a lot of noise. They rumble inside you like rioting prisoners. The more I helped my coachees to live their dreams, the more my own churned inside me.

The irony was that I had already started writing Right Risk, and, informally, had begun using the 10 Right Risk principles with my coachees. Here I was, the guy who had dived from higher than the treetops, the guy who had done some 300 dives while engulfed in flames, the guy who spent most weekends thrashing through treacherous whitewater in his kayak, utterly incapable of applying the risk principles in my own life. I rationalized that this was different, that there was a lot more at stake than just a physical risk. I didn't care how "right" this risk was. It could end up injuring my career, my reputation, and my livelihood. Heck, I could even end up losing my marriage. *Leave a high-paying job to become a writer and professional speaker?* Yeah, *that's* attractive.

Choosing Ourselves

Every person must apply the Right Risk principles in his or her own way. Think of them as navigational aids that help you become the person you want to become. My authentic destination was to become a writer, speaker, and consultant. This meant leaving the security of a good job with a reputable company. Your destination, and therefore your risk, will undoubtedly be different. Instead of detailing the specific ways in which I applied the Right Risk principles toward my risk, I am going to tell you about the very first, and most important, thing I did. The thing that makes all giant leaps possible. I MADE A CHOICE.

The Bible tells us that "many are called but few are chosen." I see it differently. I think that *all* are called, but few choose. Each of us has a calling, some worthwhile endeavor that we are *supposed* to be pursuing. But because listening to our calling takes patience and effort, and because following our calling means giving up so much, we ignore our inner longings and in the process deny ourselves. Shunning our calling, we are left with no choice but to settle for lesser dreams lived out by a less-than-authentic self. The low-frequency sadness that a lot of us feel is merely a longing for the person we are supposed to be. We miss ourselves. We miss the self denied. We were called, but we didn't choose.

To be authentic is to follow your calling and to embrace your uniqueness. Being authentic is ultimately an affirmation, an act of homage. It is saying "Yes!" to both our God and ourselves by being who we are supposed to be. For me, as much as I knew that I was denying my soul, I just couldn't choose yes. That is, until the walls came crumbling down.

The Giant Leap Decision

The turning point came in September of 2001 as I watched the Twin Towers crumble to the ground. The whole tragedy unfolded on our television monitors at work. In those brief, profane moments, like so many other Americans, I became acutely aware of life's fragility. Few things are as stark as death to make you so aware of the value of life. A good friend of mine was killed that day. We had been lifeguards together in my hometown of Larchmont, New York.

I stared out my office window for a long time that day. I was completely incensed. But the anger jostled something loose in me. Things had changed, and so had I. One thing was immediately clear to me: *Life is too short to live a compromised life*.

Right there in my small office, with the world seeming to fall apart around me, I made my giant leap decision: I WILL STOP BETRAYING MYSELF!

There were a lot of other things that I would do before taking my big risk. There would be months of preparation and applying the Right Risk principles before I left Accenture. I went on a three-day retreat and consulted my golden silence. I wrote my risk script by picking a mantra ("Trust God"). I mustered the courage to inform my boss of my decision. I trespassed beyond the wishes of all the people who implored me not to risk it (my wife was not one of them, by the way). And I exposed myself in every way possible. Applying the Right Risk principles was indispensable in helping me take my big risk. But giant leaps with your life start with giant decisions in your heart. I would not have been able to apply the principles at all had I not made the critical decision to stop betraying myself. That decision helped prioritize all the other decisions that followed, and has become the basis for all of my future risk-taking decisions.

Reaping the Rewards

Success, like wealth, is a matter of definition. I cannot tell you that my giant leap has been a financial windfall, though I have made a bit of money. But I can tell you that I am happier and more full of life. All the energy that once went into masking my true self has been redirected toward my passionate aims. I am no longer a fake, and, I believe, I am living an authentic life. Not because I am a writer, speaker, and consultant—that's what I do, not who I am. But because my dreams are no longer held hostage by my fears. I am living farther from societal preferences, and closer to my instincts.

I am living unattached to outcomes, beyond the confines of my comfort zone, wonderfully exposed.

Ultimately, giant leaps are leaps of faith. Joseph Campbell once said that when you take leaps of faith, unseen hands are there to catch you. That certainly has been true in my case. I now know that providence works if you let it. But we have to be the ones to make the first move. We have to step off the high platform.

Now It's Your Turn

Yes, the Rightest Risk of all is to be yourself, even if being yourself means losing stature, money, prestige, or the identity that others prefer. Living a life of authenticity is an act of personal fidelity. When we stop betraying ourselves, our life takes on meaning, substance, and relevance. You cannot escape the longings of your soul, nor should you. The closer you get to your authentic self, the less you diverge from your own identity. It all starts with a choice, the exercise of prerogative. Will you be who you *are*, or will you be who you are *not?*

Taking the Right Risk of authenticity means embarking on a journey of liberation, the journey of your destiny, your own personal freedom march. There are no maps, few boundaries, and plenty of hazards. Yes, you will have to give up a lot, and yes, you will suffer through hardship. You will be called to do what is uncomfortable and inconvenient, to stand alone and face your fears, and then to bring the full potency of your authenticity back into the world.

Why do it? For the same reasons you take any other Right Risk. In the struggle to overcome your fears, in the courage to face your demons, and in your willingness to take a stand for what you believe in, you build and fortify your integrity. When you risk because you feel called to do so, when you risk out of your authenticity, you risk with greater confidence and less regret. Right Risk-taking, then, is about something much more important than adrenaline, or control, or machismo. Each Right Risk becomes a projection of your character, an external manifestation of your personal theology. Thus, the greatest reward for each Right Risk taken is an intimate encounter with the magnificence of your own soul.

Notes

It's Risky Out There

1. R.D. Hershey, Jr. "The Markets: Survey Says 78.7 Million Own Stocks in United States." *The New York Times,* Friday, October 22, 1999, Section C, p. 10.

2. National Gambling Impact and Policy Commission (U.S.), *The National Gambling Impact Study Commission: Final Report.* (U.S. GPO: Superintendent of Documents, 1999).

3. "Credit Debt Problems in Australia, Britain, and Singapore." *Asia Pulse,* Canberra, September 11, 2002.

4. N. Dillon, "Debt Load an Econ Crunch, Climbing Credit Card Bills May Crimp Consumer Spending." *New York Daily News,* July 30, 2001, business section, p. 23.

5. D. Aird, "Student Credit Card Use Rockets." *The Atlanta-Journal Constitution*, July 14, 2002, section Q, p. 1.

6. K.Yoshino and C. Liu, "Thrill Rides' G-Forces Also Being Felt in Court." *Los Angeles Times*, May 27, 2002, p. 1.

7. J. Walker, "Market ends '02 in Bear's Shadow." *The Atlanta Journal-Constitution,* January 1, 2003, p. D1.

8. National Gambling Impact and Policy Commission (U.S.). *The National Gambling Impact Study Commission: Final Report.*

9. B. Gravely, "Personal Bankruptcies Set Record." *Chicago Sun-Times,* February 20, 2002, financial section, p. 59; and F. Harrop, "Economy is Full of Worst-Case Scenarios." *The Atlanta Journal-Constitution,* December 27, 2002, p. A15.

10. Consumer Product Safety Review, Winter 1999.

11. S. Greenhouse, "Americans' Lead in Work Hours Grew in 90's." *The New York Times,* July 10, 1999, late edition, final, section A, p. 8.

12. M. Jackson, "It's 5 P.M. Friday: Know Where Your Weekend Is?" *The New York Times,* March 11, 2002.

13. "Where Has All The Time Gone?" *The Atlanta Journal-Constitution,* May 12, 2002, p. A10.

14. "Yawn: These Are Such Exciting Times." *The New York Times,* February 20, 2000, section 4, p. 7.

15. D. Leeth, "Travel on the Wild Side: Risk-taking Tourists Seem Eager for Adventure After Sept. 11." *The Denver Post,* May 19, 2002, travel section, p. 1; and "Yes You!" *The Washington Post,* March 18, 2001, final edition, p. E01.

16. B. Urstadt, "Out There." *Worth,* April 2002, pp. 86–91.

17. D. France, "One Real Space Cowboy." *Newsweek,* March 21, 2001, p. 43.

18. C. Salter, "Leap of Faith." *Fast Company,* April 2002, pp. 94–99.

19. C. Grimshaw, "Living Dangerously." *Sports Marketing,* March 29, 2002, p. 35.

Right Risk

1. Joyce Baldwin, "Genetic Link Found for the Personality Trait of Novelty Seeking." *Psychiatric Times,* April 1996, vol. 13, issue 4.

2. Scott Gummer, "The Explorer's Heart." *Vanity Fair,* May 2002, pp. 100–101.

3. H. Burkholtz, "Giving Thalidomide a Second Chance." *FDA Consumer,* September 1, 1997, vol. 31.

4. Linda Bren, "Frances Oldham Kelsey: FDA Medical Reviewer Leaves Her Mark on History." *FDA Consumer Magazine,* March–April 2001.

5. Ralph Waldo Emerson, "The Over-Soul" from *Essays: First*

Series (1841) in *The Essential Writings of Ralph Waldo Emerson* edited by Bruce Atkinson (New York: Random House, 2000).

Principle 1: Find Your Golden Silence

1. Rollo May, *The Courage to Create*. (New York: W.W. Norton and Company, 1975).

2. Oprah Winfrey, "Right Now You Are One Choice Away from a New Beginning." *O Magazine*, July 2002, p. 196.

3. C. Whitehouse, "Casting Out Demons." *Time International*, July 9, 2001, vol. 158, p. 59.

4. Henry David Thoreau, *Walking*. (Bedford, MA: Applewood Books,1992).

5. Anthony de Mello, *Awareness*. (New York: Doubleday, 1992), p. 55.

6. Franz Kafka in *The Collected Aphorisms,*Vol. 1, no. 109, Shorter Works, Edited and translated by Malcolm Pasley (London: Syrens [Penguin]), 1974).

7. Anthony de Mello, *Awareness*, p. 43.

Principle 4: Turn on the Risk Pressure

1. Jill Lieber, "Pioneer Burton Riding Snowboarding Avalanche." *USA Today*, February 6, 2002, p. C8.

2. Gardiner Morse, "Innovation, Inc." *Harvard Business Review*, August 2002, pp. 18–19.

3. Bill Treasurer, "How Risk-Taking Really Works." *Training Magazine*, January 2002, pp. 40–44.

4. Nick Leeson, *Rogue Trader: How I Brought Down Barings Bank and Shook the Financial World*. (New York: Little, Brown and Company, 1996).

5. The details of this story came from several sources: Howard G. Chua-Eoan, "Going For Broke: The Ego of a 28-Year-Old Trader and the Greed of His 232-Year-Old Bank Combine to

Destroy an Investment Empire, Stunning the Business World." *Time*, March 13, 1995, p. 40; John R. Nofsinger, *Investment Blunders (of the Rich and Famous) . . . and What You Can Learn from Them.* (Upper Saddle River, NJ: Financial Times Prentice Hall, 2002); Barry Hillenbrand, "Scandals: Who Was In Charge? The Bank of England Reports That Mismanagement Allowed Nick Leeson to Break the Back of Barings." *Time International*, July 31, 1995, p. 30; D. Visser, "Trading Places." *Minneapolis Star Tribune*, July 7, 1999, p. 01D; and Leeson, *Rogue Trader*.

Principle 5: Put Yourself on the Line

1. Susan Estrich, "Rape." *Yale Law Journal 95*, 1986, p. 1087.

2. Scott Shepard, "A Year Later, Jeffords' Switch Reverberates." *The Atlanta Journal-Constitution*, May 24, 2002. p. A3.

3. Associated Press, "Study Finds Evidence of Personality Genes." *The Columbian*, May 25, 1998, world and nation section.

4. This quote is from "Interview with Dr. Jonas Salk," May 16, 1991, The Hall of Science and Exploration, Academy of Achievement. (http://www.achievement.org/autodoc/page /sal0int-1. Other sources for details in this story are Wilfrid Sheed, "Time 100: Virologist Jonas Salk; Many Scientists Were Racing to Make a Polio Vaccine in the '50s—But He Got There First." *Time*, March 29, 1999, p. 168; Michael Neill, Scott Lafee, and Mary Esselman, "Tribute: Hero in a White Lab Coat: With His Polio Vaccine, Jonas Salk Made the World a Safer Place for Children." *People*, July 10, 1995, p. 76; and D. Denenberg and L. Roscoe, "Jonas Salk: Medical Pioneer." *Lancaster New Era*, April 30, 2002, p. A-12.

5. "Hunter, John (1728–1793)" in *The Hutchinson Dictionary of Scientific Biography*, January 1, 1998.

6. R.K. Sobel, "Barry Marshall: A Gutsy Gulp Changes Medical Science." *Newsweek*, August 27, 2001, p. 59.

7. M.R. Levenson, "Risk-taking Personality." *Journal of Personality and Social Psychology*, vol 58 (6), June 1990, pp. 1073–1080.

Principle 6: Make Fear Work For You

1. http://www.af.mil/news/factsheets/Thunderbirds.html

2. Rene Sanchez, "A City Combats AIDS Complacency: As Rate of Sexual Diseases Climb, San Francisco Preaches Risk to Gay Men." *The Washington Post*, May 12, 2002, p. A03.

3. Richard W. Sterling and William C. Scott, *Plato's The Republic*. (New York: W.W. Norton and Company, 1996).

4. Michael J. Apter, *The Dangerous Edge: The Psychology of Excitement* (New York: The Free Press, a Division of Macmillan, 1992).

Principle 7: Have the Courage to Be Courageous

1. Craig Vetter, "The Immovable Object Meets the Unstoppable Force." *Outside Magazine*, December 2000.

2. Robert Sullivan (with reporting by Brad Liston, Michelle McCalope, McKenna Collette Parker), "Dale Earnhardt/The Last Lap: 1951–2001." *Time*, March 5, 2001, p. 60.

3. Sullivan, "Dale Earnhardt/The Last Lap: 1951–2001." p. 60.

4. Cora Daniels, "It's a Living Hell: Whistleblowing Makes for Great TV, But the Aftereffects Can Be Brutal." *Fortune*, April 15, 2002, pp. 367–368.

5. W. Shapiro, "FBI, Enron Memo Writers Probably Felt Similar Push." *USA Today*, May 29, 2002, p. 10A.

6. Shapiro, "FBI, Enron Memo Writers Probably Felt Similar Push," p. 10A.

7. Geoffrey Colvin, "Wonder Women of Whistleblowing." *Fortune*, August 12, 2002, p. 56.

8. Matthew Cooper, "10 Questions for Ralph Nader." *Time*, August 5, 2002, p. 6.

9. Elizabeth Mullener, "Tales of Heroism." *The Times-Picayune* (New Orleans), December 7, 2001, national section, p. 14.

10. Stephanie Salter, "Activism; Never, Never, Never Give Up; From War Hero to Pacifist." *San Francisco Chronicle*, November 4, 2001, insight section, p. C3.

11. Michael Taylor, "A Matter of Honor; He Gave Back His Medal of Honor to Risk His Freedom in Protesting His Countries Policies." *San Francisco Chronicle,* March 13, 2000, news section, p. A3.

12. Richard Whitt, "War Hero Now Wages Struggle Against Violence." *The Atlanta Journal-Constitution,* November 14, 1999, p. F5.

Principle 8: Be Perfectly Imperfect

1. Monica Ramirez Basco, *Never Good Enough* (New York: Simon and Schuster, 1999).

2. James Baldwin, *The Price of the Ticket: Collected Nonfiction 1948–1985* (New York: St. Martin's Press, 1985).

Principle 9: Trespass Continuously

1. Susan Hahn and Alison Hahn, "Educationist's Anti-Nazi Role." Independent (London), Letter to the Editors. August 27, 1994, p. 10.

2. Martin Flavin, *Kurt Hahn's Schools and Legacy.* (Wilmington, DE: The Middle Atlantic Press, 1996).

3. Carolyn Curtis, "Outward Bound." *Saturday Evening Post,* November 21, 1995, vol 267, p. 74 (3).

4. M. T. Khan, "Voyage to Maturity." *Birmingham Post,* April 4, 2001, p. 43.

5. Flavin, *Kurt Hahn's Schools and Legacy.*

6. C. P. Snow, "Either-or." *Progressive,* vol. 24, p. 535, 1961.

7. Stanley Milgram, *Obedience to Authority.* (New York: Harper and Row Publishers, 1974).

8. Peter Gray, *Psychology.* (New York: Worth Publishers, 1991).

9. Milgram, *Obedience to Authority.*

10. Thomas Blass, "The Man Who Shocked the World." *Psychology Today,* March 1, 2002, p. 68.

11. Milgram, *Obedience to Authority.*

12. Nell Boyce et al., "Hugh Thompson: Reviled, Then Honored, for His Actions at My Lai." Special issue of *U.S. News and World Report: Real Heroes.* August 20–27, 2001, pp. 33–34.

13. Rollo May, *The Courage to Create,* (New York: W.W. Norton and Company, 1975).

Principle 10: Expose Yourself

1. Don Jewel is not his real name.

2. Thomas Moore, *Soul Mates: Honoring the Mysteries of Love and Relationship.* (New York: HarperCollins Publishers, 1994), p. 23.

3. Moore, *Soul Mates,* p. 30.

The Rightest Risk of All

1. Pindar, *The Olympian and Pythian Odes;* Ralph Waldo Emerson, *Essay II: Self-Reliance;* Erich Fromm, *Man for Himself: An Inquiry into the Psychology of Ethics* (New York: Henry Holt, reprinted 1990); Robert Louis Stevenson, *Of Men and Books* (1882); Abraham Maslow, "A Theory of Human Motivation," *Psychological Review,* vol. 50, 1943, pp. 370–396.

2. M. Jenkins, "King of the Dirtbags." *Outside Magazine,* November 2001. p. 45.

3. Dante Alighieri, *The Divine Comedy:* Volume 1, *Inferno,* Canto 66 (New York: Penguin Books, 1984).

4. Ralph Waldo Emerson, "Self-Reliance" from *Essays: First Series* (1841). www.RWE.org—The Works of Ralph Waldo Emerson.

Index

Boy Scouts, Honor Medal recipients, 97–99
bravery, U.S. Congressional Medal of Honor, 124–125
breathing, composure, 119–120
British Medical Journal, thalidomide use, 35
Buckaroo Banzais, dot-com "space", 79
Buch, Paul, U.S. Congressional Medal of Honor, 125
bulldozer, vs. pavement, 2

cages, tigers, 112
calling, following your, 180
Campbell, Joseph
  finding your muse, 172
  leaps of faith, 182
capability, courage, 118–119
Captain Inferno, 5
Carpenter, Jake Burton, snowboarding, 77
Catmull, Ed (Pixar Animation), inspiring innovation, 77–78
cave dwellings, paintings, 30
challenge, meeting unexpected, 97–99
change
  behavioral, 52
  overcoming inertia, 51–52
  re-scripting, 65–66
channels, feedback, 161–162
chaos, calming inner, 44
Chemie Gruenthal, FDA approval of thalidomide, 34–36
choices
  courage, 3–4
  deviating from expected behaviors, 65
  habits that inhibit, 64
  making, 180
  prerogative, 34
  regret, 21–22
Chouinard, Yvon, Patagonia, 174–175
Christ, Jesus, acts of courage, 153
Clay, Cassius (Muhammad Ali), acts of defiance, 152
Clinton, Bill, peer pressure, 78

coaching
  instilling courage, 71–72
  job responsibilities, 173
  reaching goals, 56
Coburn, Lawrence, Soldiers Medal, 151–152
comedy, choreographed routines, 61–63
command
  defying chain of, 151–152
  obedience to chain of, 145–146
commitment, decisions, 129
complacency, success, 105–107
composure, breathing, 119–120
conditioning, skills to cope with the unexpected, 97–99
confidence
  calm, 70–71
  capability, 112
  gaining, 69–71
  lead-ups, 56
  personal convictions, 94–96
conflict, interpersonal, 159–161
conformity
  peer pressure, 78–79
  personal authenticity, 177–178
confrontation
  courage, 119–120
  fearfulness vs. fearlessness, 161
  reality assessment, 163–164
contender, achieving your potential, 57
control
  comfort zones, 57
  freak, 67
  perfectionism, 133–137
convictions
  courage of, 153
  moral, 151–152
Cooper, Cynthia, WorldCom whistleblower, 123
Copernicus, acts of defiance, 152
courage, to be courageous, 105–127
cowardice
  acts of, 118–119
  courage, 116–118
crimes, obedience, 146
criteria, right risk, 33–34, 37

danger
excitement, 111–112
fear, 105
Dante, *The Divine Comedy, Vol. I: Inferno*, 176–177
Darwin, Charles, acts of defiance, 152
De Blanc, Jefferson, U.S. Congressional Medal of Honor, 124
de Mello, Anthony
Awareness, 47
coping with emptiness, 45
death, acknowledging possibility of, 94
debriefing, group dynamics, 135–136
debt, credit card, 16
decisions
commitment, 129
giant leap, 180–181
defiance, courageous acts of, 152–153
definition, risk, 1–2, 171
deformities, thalidomide use and birth, 35–36
denial, alcoholics, 137–138
desperation, survival, 56–57
dialogue, group activities, 135–136
difficulty, degree of, 132–133
discipline, boundaries, 45
disclosure, personal, 158
disobedience, point of, 146, 149–150
dissatisfaction, purposeful anxiety, 75–76
dissidents, silencing, 124
distractions, modern lifestyles, 15–17
distrust, limiting scripts, 68
dive, first high, 23–26
diversity, nature, 174–175
diving
fear, 104
high, 4–6
dreams
buried, 179
pursuing your, 55
workaholism, 54
dynamics, group, 134–137

Earnhardt, Dale, NASCAR driver, 122
Edison, Thomas, failed experiments, 132
education, adventure-based, 144–145
effect
double or nothing, 85–86
Fall Hike, 125–126
mere exposure, 108
once bitten, 85
Eliot, T. S., creative endeavors, 92
Emerson, Ralph Waldo
capitulation to authority, 143
conformity, 177–178
courage, 115
personal integrity, 173
sacred vs. literary teachers, 36
emotions, volatility, 158
emptiness, coping with, 45
endorsements, product, 80–82
engagment, emotional, 166–167
Enron, accounting whistleblower, 123
Estrich, Susan, rape victim advocacy, 95–96
Everest, Ed Viesturs, 121
evil, obedience, 146, 148–149
evolution, from one persona to another, 96–97
excitement, danger, 111–112
executives, behavioral latitude, 162
exercises
assessing your courage level, 126–127
exposing yourself, 167–168
Finding Your Golden Silence, 48–49
harnessing your fears, 113–114
overcoming inertia, 57–59
perfect imperfection, 141–142
personal tolerance, 101–102
pressure tolerance, 88–89
script creation, 73
trespassing continuously, 154
expectation, shifting from gain to loss, 81–82
experimentation, fearless, 64–65
exposure, personal, 155–168

Index

About the Author

Bill Treasurer is a writer, speaker, consultant, and founder of Giant Leap Consulting, Inc., an organizational development company whose motto is *Daring to Excel*. From 1996–2002, Treasurer was a consultant with Accenture, a large management and technology consulting company. After working in the areas of executive communications and change management, Treasurer became a full-time internal executive coach on Accenture's largest client engagement. Prior to joining Accenture, Bill was a vice president at Executive Adventure Inc., an Atlanta-based team-building company where he facilitated corporate team-building events. He began his consulting career at High Performing Systems Inc., where he designed and delivered leadership and team development programs.

Treasurer has worked with over 75 prominent organizations in the area of organizational development, leadership, change management, and team-building. He holds a Masters Degree in Administrative Science, with a concentration in OD, from the University of Wisconsin Green Bay. His undergraduate education is from West Virginia University, where he attended school on a full athletic scholarship.

Treasurer is a former member of the U.S. High Diving Team—a troupe of aquatic entertainers. From 1984–1991 Treasurer performed some 1,500 high dives from heights that soared to over 100 feet. His risk-taking exploits have been published in *Training Magazine* and ASTD's *T & D Magazine*.

Treasurer is active in the prevention of both substance abuse and child abuse. Though he no longer high dives, Bill is an avid whitewater kayaker. He lives in Decatur, Georgia with his wife, Shannon, and their dog Gulliver.

To contact Bill Treasurer about speaking to your organization, go to www.giantleapconsulting.com.